Praise for
On My Own Two Feet

"Amy Purdy is far more than an Olympic champion. She is a pioneer and a beacon of strength. Her honest and sharply written memoir leaves me feeling as uplifted as I do when I spend time in her presence." —Elizabeth Gilbert, author of *Eat, Pray, Love*

"Amy Purdy is the true definition of what it means to defy the odds. I stand in awe of Amy's determination, bravery, and grace. As phenomenal as the woman who wrote it, her memoir is a gift worth reading, rereading, and sharing with many others."

—Derek Hough, author of *Taking the Lead*

"In *On My Own Two Feet,* Amy not only demonstrates resilience in the face of calamity, she also shares a set of spiritual principles that reawakens us to our potential for endless growth. What a remarkable young woman—and what a gem of a book."

—Deepak Chopra

On My Own Two Feet

On My Own Two Feet

*From Losing My Legs
to Learning the Dance of Life*

AMY PURDY
with Michelle Burford

wm

WILLIAM MORROW
An Imprint of HarperCollins*Publishers*

This book is dedicated to the dreamers.

All photographs courtesy of the author except where noted.

HarperCollins books may be purchased for educational, business, or sales promotional use. For information please e-mail the Special Markets Department at SPsales@harpercollins.com.

A hardcover edition of this book was published in 2014 by William Morrow, an imprint of HarperCollins Publishers.

FIRST WILLIAM MORROW PAPERBACK EDITION PUBLISHED 2015.

Designed by Lisa Stokes

Library of Congress Cataloging-in-Publication Data has been applied for.

ISBN 978-0-06-237910-8

17 18 19   OV/RRD   10 9 8 7 6 5 4

Contents

Prologue

If your life were a book and you were the author, how would you want your story to go? In 1999 during one of the most challenging moments I had ever faced, I asked myself that question. The path that led me to that defining question—and the many worlds I've experienced on the other side of it—is a story I've only shared with my close friends and family. Until now.

Years before I first cha-cha'd onto the stage of *Dancing with the Stars,* I had an instinct—a strong feeling in my gut that whispered, "There's something more for you to do." That inkling has carried me from my childhood in the scorching Las Vegas Valley to a snowcapped mountain in Sochi, Russia. Along the way, I've experienced every intense emotion you can imagine: Exhaustion. Exhilaration. Devastation. Bliss. Heartbreak. Discouragement.

Jubilation. I've also traveled to places that even a dreamer like me could not have envisioned. It's been a wild ride—and this book is my memory of it.

This is more than just an account of my life. It's the story of my spiritual journey—one I'm still navigating on my own two feet. As you read through these pages, I hope the same lightbulb moments that have lit my way will bring you some similar insights: That each of us is far more capable than we could ever know. That what at first seems like a detour could turn out to be your destiny. That if you can just practice shifting your viewpoint, an overwhelming challenge can start looking more like a beautiful blessing. I am the living, breathing, dancing proof of that.

These days, many people stop me on the street and say, "You're an inspiration"—and I'm always humbled by their words and grateful for their admiration. But the truth is that I don't want to simply offer others a fleeting moment of "inspiration." I want my story to spark real change. An *aha* moment becomes most meaningful when it leads us to do more. Dream bigger. Move past our so-called limitations. Defy expectations. Bounce back with the resilience that every single one of us was born with. I didn't write this book because I want you to say, "Wow, look at what that girl overcame—good for her." I'm sharing my story because I want you to see what's possible in your own life. Right here. Right now. Starting the second you pick up your pen and create your own amazing narrative.

The words of the Chinese philosopher Lao-tzu have always resonated with me: "A journey of a thousand miles begins with a single step." What follows is my first step. My first stumble. My first dance. My first dream.

CHAPTER 1

The Stranger

"It is only with the heart that one can see rightly;
what is essential is invisible to the eye."
—ANTOINE DE SAINT-EXUPÉRY

June 1999—Las Vegas, Nevada

My day was over. Finally. Since that morning, I'd been working at my dream job—as a massage therapist in a world-class spa called Canyon Ranch. As passionate as I was about my work there, I was thrilled to be finished that evening. So at the end of my shift, I quickly cleaned and organized my room. I then began the long walk out of the massive spa, through the Venetian hotel and casino, and—at last—to my car. Just as I got off the elevator that led to the parking garage, my cell phone rang. It was my manager, Shane.

"Amy, are you still on the property?"

"Um, yes—I'm still here," I said. "What's up?"

"Can you come back and do a massage?" My throat tightened. I peered out over the rows of cars, squinting to spot my blue Toyota pickup. "We have this client, and he has somehow been forgotten about," Shane continued. "He's been sitting in the lounge area for a while. There's nobody who's free to massage him now."

"Oh, really?" I said, buying time so I could think of a way to get out of it. I paused, drew in a sharp breath, and swallowed hard. "Well," I said, "I guess I could come back and take him. It's just one more hour." *Crap.*

Turning back was the last thing I wanted to do. All day, I'd been looking forward to hanging out with friends. It was hot—112 degrees that day—and I was wiped. But I did feel sorry for the guy; he'd already been waiting forever. "I'll be there in a few minutes," I told Shane. I then let out a loud sigh and turned around to make the trek all the way back through the entire hotel and casino: Through a series of hallways. Through the noisy casino. Through the hotel. And, finally, into the spa.

All the rooms in the spa were in use that evening—so Shane set up a table for me in an unfinished room; because the spa was brand-new, some of the rooms weren't yet complete. Once I had everything ready, I walked out to the lounge to meet the man. He was an older guy, probably seventy, with tan, leathered skin, high cheekbones, and crystal-blue eyes. He looked part Native American. In every line on his face, you could read the experience that seemed written there.

"How are you?" I said, extending my hand. He stood and took me by the palm; his hands were soft and warm. "I'm good," he said. He had the sweetest smile on his face—so pleasant—and all at once, I was happy I'd come back for such a nice guy. "Follow me this way," I said, leading him toward the room. Once we got inside, I told him the same thing I told all my clients: "I'll start you with your face down." I pointed toward the face cradle on the table, and he nodded. I then left the room so he could change.

There are times when you massage someone, and it feels like the person's body is resisting your touch. This man's body was the exact opposite. From the moment I laid my palms on his upper back, I could feel his breath; my hands seemed to melt right into him—like there was no separation between my palms and his body. His skin was warm, and his muscles were pliable and accepting. "Wow, you have an amazing touch," he said. "I can tell you're an intuitive person." Pause. "Thanks," I said. I smiled and continued kneading his back in silence.

I rarely talked to my clients—I respected the fact that many people want to lie there and decompress in total quiet. But this man clearly wanted to talk, and over the next half hour, he told me all kinds of things about his life. His family. His work. I mostly listened, throwing in a few words here and there. Yet as little as I said in response, he seemed to keep going deeper and deeper in the conversation.

"You're going to go on and do amazing things in your life," he told me. "I can feel it by your presence."

I remained quiet for a moment. "Really?" I said.

"Yes," he answered. "You seem so connected."

At this point, I'd been a massage therapist for several months. During that time, I'd heard all kinds of stuff—you wouldn't believe some of the things people reveal once they get comfortable. So I'd learned how to stay focused on the massage and not get caught up in long discussions. But for some reason, my conversation with this man was different—his words actually resonated with me. My lower lids filled with water. "Your life is going to change in a big way," he continued. "I can tell."

I gasped. For a couple of years, I'd been carrying around this unexplainable feeling in my gut—a sense that something huge was about to happen to me. I had no idea where the feeling came from, or whether it signaled something good or bad—but it was an anticipation that grew stronger with each passing day. I didn't know whether this man's words had anything to do with that feeling, but I had an eerie sense that I should pay close attention. I leaned in and pressed my warm fingertips deeper into his back.

A few minutes before our session ended, the man asked me a question out of nowhere. He first cleared his throat. "Have you crossed over to the other side yet?" I stopped massaging for a half second, gently resting my palms on his calves. As weird as the question was, I kind of knew what he meant. "No," I finally said. "But I do feel like something's going to happen in my life—and I don't know what it is."

"Well," he said, adjusting his body down a bit on the table, "I crossed over when I was young." When he was a teenager, he explained, he fell down a well and into a pool of water and nearly drowned; rescuers pulled him out and struggled to resuscitate him. "I actually stopped breathing," he said. "I went to the other side." Long pause. "And when I came back," he finally continued, "the surface life I'd been living was completely different from the deeper life I lived afterward. I was living on a totally different vibration."

At this point, the few trickles of water on my lids became a stream of tears. I tried to squelch them, but huge drops spilled from my eyes and splattered down onto the man's legs. My strong reaction surprised me—I'd never become emotional while giving a client a massage. Never. "I think the same thing is going to happen to you one day," he said. He paused, then exhaled loud enough for me to hear it. "And when it does happen—don't be scared." I nodded but didn't say a word.

A few moments later, the massage was finished. Once the man got dressed, I returned to his room to escort him back to the waiting area. I didn't usually hug my clients—but because we'd shared this incredible connection, we embraced. Embracing each other somehow felt right.

I didn't meet up with my friends after all that night. Instead, I slid into the front seat of my truck and drove myself home in silence. As I turned onto the dirt road that led up to my house, I replayed the conversation in my head. Against the hush of the Vegas desert, the man's final words seemed to reverberate over and over: *Don't be scared. Don't be scared. Don't be scared.* Once I got inside the house and settled into my room, I wrote down his words in my journal.

When you're nineteen, everything feels possible. I had my whole life ahead of me. I was strong and independent. I had a job I loved, I made good money at it, and I had big plans to save up and travel the world. The idea that I would ever be "scared" of anything—whatever it was, whenever it might come—wasn't something I even thought about. My only two worries in life were whether I'd shaved my legs or gained any weight. There I was, standing tall at the start of my journey, and I was pretty sure how I wanted the adventure to turn out. I couldn't have known that on a sweltering night in June—in a mysterious conversation with a stranger—part of my story had already been written. Our meeting was the very first chapter.

CHAPTER 2

Desert Daydreams

"I only ask to be free. The butterflies are free."
—CHARLES DICKENS

I've always had a wild imagination. When I was five, I'd gather up my Barbies—the ones with the eighties Madonna haircut I'd given them—and sit under our massive pomegranate tree in the backyard. Behind the tree, I spotted a tiny white door. "Where do you think that goes?" I'd ask my dolls. I'm pretty sure it led to our neighbors' yard. But in my eyes, it had to be a secret doorway, a passageway to a magical kingdom. I thought, *I bet Alice in Wonderland lives behind that door.* That's the kind of daydreamer I was.

My family lived in a three-bedroom house on Bonita Avenue. When you say you're from Vegas, people assume you grew up surrounded by the bright lights of the Strip. I didn't. We weren't far from the Strip, but my neighborhood, which was in old Vegas, seemed a world away: grassy lawns, big trees, little parks. It was close to the same area where my dad grew up; his parents, my Grandma and Grandpa Purdy, lived ten minutes from us.

I didn't know much about our neighbors. That's the culture in Vegas: People can live next door to each other and rarely talk. I mostly played with my sister, Crystal, who's about two years older than me. I also had some family in town; both my parents are the eldest of three. My mother, Sheri, has two sisters, Cindy and Debbie; my dad, Stef, has a brother, Stan, and a sister, Cindy—yep, we have two Cindys in our family. So I grew up with cousins who felt more like siblings: Michelle (Aunt Debbie's eldest child, who's four years younger than me, and the one cousin I spent the most time with); Jack and Shannon (also Debbie's kids); and finally, my much younger cousin, Jessica, who's the only child of my mom's sister, Cindy. My uncle Stan, who once worked as a bodyguard for celebs like Michael Jackson, Will Smith, and Vin Diesel, never had kids. Neither did my dad's late sister, Cindy.

Our home was filled with music. My parents had a huge collection of vinyl, including classic rock (Queen, Led Zeppelin, Janis Joplin, the Eagles) and country (George Strait, Johnny Cash, Merle Haggard, Willie Nelson, and just about every song the Judds ever sang). My dad would often put on his *Big Chill* soundtrack and dance around all silly to "Heard It Through the Grapevine." Or he'd play "My Girl" and sing it to me and Crystal. He didn't have a very good voice, and he'd purposely try to embarrass us by dropping us off at school in his big blue Bronco, turning up "My Girl" on the radio and getting out of the car to sing. Crystal couldn't stand it. I was amused.

When we weren't with my mom's parents, Grandma and Grandpa Campbell, we spent a lot of time with my aunt Debbie.

She once lived in Vail, Colorado, which is where she met my uncle Rich. "What's Vail like?" I was always asking her. "It was beautiful," she'd tell me, smiling at the memory. "We'd stay outdoors all day and ski, and then go out at night and have so much fun. It was the kind of town where everyone knew everyone." I was captivated. *What would it be like to live up in the mountains and play in the snow all day?* My aunt Cindy also once lived in the mountains in Aspen, Colorado. "I'd be out going for a run and see a bear right in the middle of the road!" she told me. Fascinating.

After my aunt and uncle left Vail, they moved to Australia for a while. "I'm digging my way to Aunt Debbie on the other side of the world!" I used to tell my mom as I played in my sandbox. They eventually moved back to Vegas, and my aunt began working as a nurse; my uncle became this big-time architect—in other words, Uncle Rich was rich! That meant he and my aunt had a big house, a grand piano, and—hello—a pool. Crystal, my cousins, and I spent *hours* in that pool, playing Shark (my cousin Jack, one of the only boys in the family, always got the job of the shark who was trying to catch the rest of us!) and Marco Polo. If you're not chilling out in a pool during a Vegas summer, there's not much else you can do outside. It's just too damn hot—as in 115 degrees or even higher.

As summers drew to a close, I became more and more excited for the start of school. I went to the same school my father once attended—John S. Park Elementary—and my favorite subject was science. I've always been intrigued by how things worked (when I was really young I could sit in our garage for hours, trying out every tool in my dad's toolbox). "What do you want to be when you grow up?" Grandpa Purdy often asked me. "I want to be an astronomer or a veterinarian!" I'd announce.

When my parents saw how into science I was, they got me a subscription to *National Geographic*. For six years, I collected every single issue. I'd open one of our closets, and—flop!—dozens of copies would come toppling out. For an entire afternoon, I'd pore over the colorful photos, wondering what it would be like to visit Africa, New Zealand, Japan, Alaska—or anyplace outside of dusty Nevada. I never connected with my home state. It was too hot, too plain, too brown—too boring.

My other favorite subject was art. I could paint and get so lost in my head that I wasn't sure how much time had passed. "That's fantastic, Amy," my third-grade art teacher, Miss Bowman, would say after I finished a drawing. She was the sweetest, most down-to-earth teacher I'd ever met. She also had a daughter around my age, and along with a few other kids from school we would sometimes have sleepovers at her place. "Hello, my dear!" she'd exclaim whenever I visited. To be honest, I was better friends with Miss Bowman than I was with her daughter. She was creative: She spun her own wool and made sweaters and blankets. She had goats. And she was from Michigan, which sounded fascinating to me, simply because it wasn't Nevada.

NEITHER OF MY parents were born in Vegas. My dad is originally from Twin Falls, Idaho; Mom was born in Grand Junction, Colorado. Dad was six months old when his family moved to Vegas; Mom was already nine. So they pretty much grew up in Nevada. Even as a child, Mom was the polite, responsible type—a good girl. Early in her life, she knew she wanted to be a mother and homemaker. My father was a natural leader—outgoing, good-looking, confident.

After high school, Dad went to Vietnam. He joined the legendary 2nd Battalion 9th Marines. While out in the jungle, my father caught malaria—twice! The second time, he almost died from it and was forced to come home. Once back in Nevada, he refused to take any VA benefits. That's a perfect example of the kind of man my dad still is: He prides himself on being able to take care of things himself. Not until years later did I understand the effect it had on my dad to come home to a country that frowned on him because so many didn't agree with the war.

Once home from Vietnam, Dad went into full-tilt party mode. He grew his thick, brown mane down to his shoulders and socialized his way around Vegas and beyond. One spring afternoon, he went to a friend's wedding that my mother and her sister, Debbie, happened to be at. Dad was a friend of the groom, and Mom was a friend of the bride. My mom was immediately attracted to my dad, but my father initially had his eye on Debbie. Later, when my dad called asking for Debbie (long story short, he needed to apologize for throwing up in Mom and Debbie's car on the way from the reception), my mom answered the phone—and the rest is history. Dad ended up asking my mom out during that call, and just three months after they met at that wedding, they were engaged themselves. They married soon after.

My parents weren't actually hippies when they lived in Lake Tahoe—but they definitely looked the part. In a faded photo that hung in our living room, Mom had on this cool rabbit fur top and bell-bottom pants, and sunglasses; Dad, who had his shirt unbuttoned down past his chest, wore a leather belt, bell-bottom jeans, and a cowboy hat. Every time I looked at that picture, I'd imagine the two of them up there in the mountains, madly in love and living this carefree life. It was exactly the kind of life I dreamed of one day having myself.

By the time Crystal came along in 1978, my parents had moved back to Vegas and bought the house on Bonita. On November 7, 1979, I made my grand entrance. "Back then, the doctors would try to tell the gender of the child by the heartbeat," my mother recalls. Mom says my heartbeat was so strong that she and the doctors were sure I was going to be a boy! "I had already decided that whether it was a boy or a girl," says Mom, "I would name the child Lane—because that's my husband's middle name." But when my mother held me in her arms for the first time, she didn't think I looked like a Lane. I looked more like an Amy.

From the time Crystal and I were both small, both my parents worked. Hard. When I was in elementary school, my mother— who had these gorgeous green eyes, amazing skin, and the perfect hourglass figure with a tiny waist—had a job as a registrar in an emergency room; later, when I was around ten, she took a high-pressure job in health insurance sales. For a few years early in my childhood, my dad was a pit boss at the New Frontier hotel and casino—he oversaw the craps tables during the night shift. "Hi, Dad!" I'd yell out, running to hug my father when he came home from work. My father was tall and lean with dark, wavy hair, high cheekbones, and blue eyes the color of the sky—in other words, the most handsome guy I'd ever seen. After work, his leather jacket smelled like cigarette smoke from spending all that time in the pit. "Come here, Amers!" Dad would say, sweeping me into his strong arms; whenever he'd kiss me on the cheek, I felt the whiskers of his dark brown mustache against my face.

Amers—that's what my dad called me. The rest of my family gave me another nickname: Amelia. They started calling me that after my mom put my hair in two braids and then pinned the braids to the top of my head. "You look like an Amelia!" my grandma said one day—and I have no idea why. But in a way, the name fit me perfectly—just like the most famous Amelia, the first woman to fly solo across the Atlantic, I was free-spirited. Creative. Adventurous. And always wondering what other worlds existed outside of Vegas.

My dad eventually left his job at the casino to become the executive director of the Helldorado rodeo, the biggest rodeo west of the Mississippi. Dad's father, Grandpa Ralph Purdy, had had the very same job earlier in his life. During a huge annual festival called "Helldorado Days," Dad oversaw the rodeo and a parade; our whole family drove downtown to the arena to catch the action. "You ready, cowgirl?" Dad would ask. "I'm ready!" I said, jumping up from my spot on the couch. Crystal and I were usually outfitted in our little cowgirl dresses and hats. I'm pretty sure my hat was a bit tilted—it's hard keeping a cowboy hat on over two Amelia braids.

My mom was Supermom. Literally. As busy as she was with her work, she woke up every morning at five o'clock and worked out on her NordicTrack in the garage while listening to Queen's "Another One Bites the Dust" or Michael Jackson's "Beat It." She had on the full getup: purple tights, pink thong leotard with a belt, blue leg warmers, and a braid and headband. Every night, she also made dinner for us; most evenings, we all sat down together around the table. That was our time to catch up over my mom's delicious meals.

Mom found all sorts of little ways to make Crystal and me feel special. "It's raining today!" she'd burst into my bedroom to announce on a morning when the sky was filled with gray rain clouds. Just hearing that sentence was enough to make my mouth water, because I knew what was coming: Whenever it rained, Mom made us chocolate chip cookies. Even now, I love a rainy day—I can almost smell the chocolate aroma wafting through the house. We did a lot of cooking and baking in my family; thanks to my mom, grandma, and aunts, I became excellent at making pies, cakes, and cookies. Even now on rainy days, my sister and I make chocolate chip cookies. It has become a tradition.

In the early part of my childhood, I attended church. My dad's parents were what some call "Jack Mormon"—meaning a Mormon who doesn't necessarily follow all the rules of the faith and lifestyle. Even though my grandparents weren't devout, they still attended church regularly—and when Crystal and I were small, they took us with them at least a couple of Sundays a month. My parents encouraged that, mostly for three reasons: They wanted us to spend time with our grandparents, they wanted to instill some morals in us and at least give us a spiritual foundation—and they needed a day off.

I hated going to church. The old, square building smelled dusty. The whole scene was drab: beige carpets, dull colors, totally boring. The hymns we sang to the sound of the pipe organ seemed dated. You know that hand-clapping, tambourine-shaking service you might find in a Baptist church? Well, let me tell you: My grandparents' church was the exact opposite. It felt like being at a funeral! To get through the two-hour yawner, I colored the whole time. The only good thing was that I got to see my grandparents, whom I loved. "You okay, honey?" my Grandma Purdy, who had red hair and my same Irish porcelain skin, would whisper to me. I nodded—and then looked around for any sign that the service would be over soon. But you want to hear something crazy? As much as I resisted going, I somehow always felt good afterward. The people were always friendly and I left feeling loved.

When you turn eight, you can be baptized into the Mormon faith. My parents gave us a choice. "Do you want to be baptized, Crystal?" Dad asked my sister right after she'd celebrated her eighth birthday. "Yes," she said with zero hesitation. "I do." When my turn rolled around, Dad asked me the same question. "There are so many different religions," I said, "so how do I know which one to pick? I only know about this one." In school, I'd run across kids who were all different types of traditions—Christian, Catholic, Muslim, Hindu. Even at such a young age, I somehow knew that I was in this little bubble—and I didn't want to commit my life to something until I'd looked into all my other options. I never wanted to be boxed in—and I'm still exactly that way. "You're my little butterfly," my mother would tell me. "You go from one thing to the next."

Mom was right. Growing up, all I could think about was being free. I wanted to escape the Vegas desert and float away to worlds more amazing than even those I'd imagined. I wanted to have great stories to tell, just like my aunts. I wanted to drift and explore and just let myself be carried away by the wind. I've since come to realize that the wind can carry you—just not always to the places you were planning to go.

OUR FAMILY WAS pretty outdoorsy. At least a few times in the summer, Dad would load up his truck and take us camping in the mountains (I still live for the smell of the pine trees and a s'more over a crackling campfire!), water skiing at Lake Mead, boogie-boarding at the beach in California, or snow skiing up at Mount Charleston.

I also spent my share of time on skis. Both my parents are skiers, so they took us on ski trips because they hoped we'd enjoy the sport as much as they do. My father would drive us three hours away to Brian Head Resort in southern Utah—Brian Head is still one of my family's favorite spots. When I was in elementary school, my dad taught me how to snow ski and water ski, but even after countless lessons on the snow, I never really got the hang of it; many times, I'd be skiing down the mountain and my skis would get all crossed up together and I'd tumble down the slope! There I was, skis twisted up like a pretzel in the snow, freezing my hands and butt off, tears frozen to my face. "Amy, pull yourself together!" my father would yell down like an army sergeant. How embarrassing.

Before I could lift myself off the ground and end my suffering, I caught a glimpse of something out of the corner of my right eye: *Swoosh!* A kid flew right past me on a snowboard. That was the first time I'd seen a snowboarder. Snowboarding seemed so effortless, and like the coolest thing in the world. Right then I looked up at my father and shouted, "Screw skiing—I'm learning to snowboard!" Dad frowned a bit and shook his head. "Well, you're never going to learn to snowboard until you learn to ski," he said. How wrong he was.

CHAPTER 3

Bonfires and Snowboards

"A girl should be two things: who and what she wants."
—COCO CHANEL

A ren't you Crystal Purdy's younger sister?" That's a question I'd heard enough of by the time I got to high school. Don't get me wrong: My sister and I are close—always have been. Aside from my parents, I'll never have a better friend and supporter. But when you're awkward and skinny and trying to figure out who the heck you are, it's not easy being two school grades behind a sister who seems so dang perfect.

My sister fell into her group of friends early—by seventh grade, she was already one of the popular kids. She was also gorgeous: Long blond hair. Tanned complexion. And my mom's awesome body, complete with the tiny waist. In high school, she became even more popular: Not only was she an A student, but she was varsity head cheerleader and the homecoming queen. She often wore cute dresses to school and she didn't drink or cuss. And as far back as I can recall, she knew what she wanted to do with her life: grow up, get married, have kids, and live in a house with a white picket fence. She had her whole life figured out and was working toward that.

Enter me, with untamed reddish hair; a bit disheveled much of the time; a bit of a wild streak and mostly sporting vintage or thrift store jeans with flip-flops or Vans. At the start of high school, I wasn't sure exactly where I belonged. Which group could I feel comfortable in? That was the question.

At times while I was still sorting that out, I borrowed Crystal's clothes. She *hated* that. But even when I wore her stuff, it didn't feel like me. I even tried to shop at the stores in the mall where she shopped—places like Contempo Casuals—but I couldn't find any outfits I liked. My classmates had always thought of me as "cool" and "creative," the kind of girl who got along with everyone. Yet when I got to Cimarron Memorial High School, I was mostly known as one thing: Crystal Purdy's little sister.

Freshman year was tough. Following in Crystal's footsteps, I tried out for the freshman cheerleading squad. When I told Crystal I was planning to try out, she just kinda shrugged. "Okay," she said, doing her best to sound encouraging, "go for it, if that's really what you want to do." I, along with about five other girls, began memorizing a choreographed routine. I don't recall the routine or even the song, but I do know that we worked on it for a few weeks that summer. Finally, the afternoon arrived when we had to perform before the coaches.

"Are you ready, girls?" a coach yelled out. We got in position. The music began—and all I can tell you is that the next five minutes were a blur. I danced like I'd been set on fire! While the other girls pranced around in perfect rhythm, I could barely control my limbs. I'd had a growth spurt the year before, and at 108 pounds and a little under five feet six, I was totally lanky and uncoordinated. For the life of me, I couldn't keep my wrists straight. I also had this crazy smile plastered all over my face, all teeth and no lips. I smiled so long my cheeks hurt. It was a complete disaster, and apparently, the coaches agreed: All the girls made the team except for one—me.

At least there was one place where I always fit—art class. I loved my art teacher, Miss Lyle, as much as I'd loved Miss Bowman. She was so encouraging: "Your paintings are good, Amy," she'd tell me, eyeing one of the sunsets or landscapes I'd created; for reasons that I'm sure you can guess by now, most of my artwork was inspired by nature.

It was in Miss Lyle's class that I heard about a group of guys I knew from around campus—the skateboarders: Brad, Richard, Aaron. Miss Lyle was always talking about the funny things they did—like when Aaron dared Brad to drink a can of paintbrush water, and yes, he drank it! In addition to being a ton of fun, they were creative: They loved art. They loved music. They didn't take themselves too seriously. The guys lived in the same neighborhood as some of my girlfriends, and when I'd go visit my friends after school, the guys would be out skateboarding. We'd dress up all cute and go watch them—and a little at time, I got to know them.

Richard and I had a crush on each other. When I was in seventh grade, I'd started to get into boys. My first kiss was with this kid named Jeremy. He was cute, blond, tall, and even lankier than me. We started hanging out and ended up really liking each other—and one day while we were by the lockers, he leaned in and kissed me. I don't remember much about Jeremy, but I do remember that I wanted to *keep* kissing him. That opened the floodgates, and I kissed many other boys after that!

Richard was stunning—six feet four, athletic, olive skin, dark hair, pretty eyes, beautiful smile. He was a senior when I was a freshman. Not many girls paid attention to him at the beginning of the school year, but by the end of it, he was definitely seen as a hottie. Plus, he was funny and really mellow. Brad was also hot: He had a smaller build, about five nine, and thin, yet he also had an athletic body. He had dark hair, brown eyes, a strong nose—a really unique look to him; he was also known as the best skate-boarder and snowboarder in school. Through Brad and Richard, I met a lot of other skaters around school. They seemed to be friends with everyone.

Richard and I hung out the most, and he talked nonstop about snowboarding. Like me, he'd been escaping to Brian Head in southern Utah for most of his life. "We drive over there and snow-board all the time," he told me. "The snow is amazing! You should go with us sometimes." I nodded, and I thought of that kid who'd flown by me on a snowboard the year before. I also thought of how cool it would be to take a trip with a hottie. Ooh-la-la.

THE GUYS WEREN'T my only friends. I also hung out with Jina, Juliette, and Talia. I first met Jina in seventh grade; she was the kind of girl who was always up for a wild adventure. Our dads worked together at the rodeo; we'd go down to the horse arena and do the great job we'd been given of shoveling horse poop. I met

Juliette and Talia toward the end of ninth grade. Juliette felt very similar to me—she was an artist and a painter. Talia always had a supercool style. Every day, she put together a new outfit that was always a mix of modern and vintage. She was five ten and thin, so her clothes always looked great on her.

The three of us went to a lot of desert parties together—those were big back then. For high school kids in Vegas, there weren't too many options for socializing, so among the skaters and the musicians, there was this culture of meeting out in the desert at night, building bonfires, and listening to music. Over the summer, underground punk rock bands from California would come through. It was all word of mouth: Someone at school would say, "Hey, you headed out to the party on Saturday night?" There would sometimes be hundreds of us, pulled up in our cars, building bonfires and hanging out in the backs of trucks, listening to music. There was always a beer keg around somewhere, or a bottle of cheap Boone's Farm wine.

When we were old enough to drive (I got my learner's permit at fifteen), my girlfriends and I piled into the beat-up red Chevy Blazer that Dad bought for Crystal and me. The two of us drove that thing so much that we used red duct tape (we wanted to match the truck!) to keep the taillights from falling off. It didn't matter how far we had to drive to get to a desert party. We were always up for the adventure. My skater guy friends usually met us out there. Wherever you find punk rock, you almost always find hot skaters.

While the punk bands played, my friends and I—gazing up at the massive sky filled with countless stars—would often get into deep conversations around the crackling bonfire.

"Do you believe in God?" Juliette once asked me.

"I don't know," I said, "but I believe *something* is out there."

"What about other dimensions?" she asked.

"Probably," I said, shrugging a little. "I've just always had this feeling that there's something bigger out there, something we can't see."

Even when I was small, I was curious about how the universe worked—and as I got into junior high and high school, I became even more curious. I read books on quantum physics and spirituality. By the time I was sixteen, Wayne Dyer and Deepak Chopra were two of my favorite authors. In church when I was small, I'd heard about God as our Heavenly Father. But I didn't believe God was just sitting up there in the clouds. To me, it seemed like God had to be bigger than that. That what religion called "God" was really a creative life force that connects everything.

I also didn't relate to all the rules that were part of religion, like that if you did something bad, you wouldn't go to heaven. I believed in compassion for others and forgiveness for mistakes—not in this judgmental God who was waiting for us all to mess up. Aside from that, I felt more in touch with God when I was in nature than I did when I was sitting in a church. I always thought there was so much going on that we couldn't see with our human eyes—and that what we think we know for certain could truly be a mystery.

"WANNA GO SNOWBOARDING with us on Saturday?" Richard asked one February afternoon in the second semester of my freshman year. Practically before he could ask, I replied, "Of course!" I was dying to try it. And it didn't hurt that I'd be learning this new sport with two of the cutest guys in school. Hey, what motivates, right?

When I first asked Mom and Dad if I could go, they were a little hesitant. "Who are you going with?" Dad asked. "A few of the guys—but Beth is going, too." Beth Riesgraf, who was really my sister's age, hung out with me a lot, too . . . we just clicked. Mentioning that Beth was going was my magic ticket. Plus, by the time I put in my request, I'd been hanging out with these guys for months. My parents had met them all, felt comfortable with them, and knew they were decent kids. "We'll be fine," I insisted. And without too much arm-twisting, my parents agreed to let me go.

Saturday morning finally arrived. In the distance, I spotted Aaron's Bronco rolling through the desert toward my house. By this time, we'd moved to an amazing adobe-style home my dad built way out to the northwest of the city. I stepped into the yard and waited. Aaron pulled into the driveway and rolled down the window, the sound of music blaring. They'd already picked up Beth; she waved at me and smiled from her backseat window. "You ready?" Aaron yelled out over the music. I nodded. Aaron threw my bag into the trunk with all the snowboard gear, and I piled into the back next to Beth. Off we sped for the next three hours, weaving through mountains and snow, blasting Metallica. It was exciting to just be outdoors. With my friends. Out of hot Vegas.

At last, we arrived and unpacked our stuff. Once we got up near the chairlifts, I strapped my left boot into the binding on the snowboard; you leave one foot free so you can skate through the lift line and push off with the back foot. "Let's go down through the trees today," I overheard Aaron say to Richard, which made me suddenly aware that I had no idea what the heck I was doing.

But there I was, this nervous young girl trying to keep up with all of the cool guys, so I stayed quiet and tried not to make a fool of myself. Brad and Richard took a spot on the chairlift, and I—heart pounding!—sat right in the center of them. *No complaints here.* The board, attached tightly to my foot, dangled beneath me.

When you ski, you get off the chairlift while facing forward, but in snowboarding, you actually get off sideways. I didn't know that, which is why—*flop!*—I fell down right away as I got off the lift. "You okay?" asked Richard. I nodded, stood up without a word, and shook it off. "We're gonna start with this hill," he said—and by "hill," he didn't mean the bunny slope. We were on the steepest run! "Just follow us!" he said. The guys strapped their back feet onto their boards and took off down the run. Beth stayed back with me to practice for a few minutes, but then she caught up with the guys. I could've asked them all to wait, but I didn't want to be the one who couldn't keep up.

Once I got my back foot securely attached to the board, I quickly got into the position I'd seen the others in: Knees slightly bent. Back straight. Body facing sideways but head looking forward toward the nose of the board. I put some pressure on my front foot to get the board moving down the mountain. Gravity soon took over, and the momentum practically pulled me down the mountain. *Thump! Thump! Thump!* My heart leapt from my chest as I suddenly began moving down the run.

Adrenaline surged through my veins. I pointed my board straight and just went! It was pretty scary to be going so fast, especially not knowing how to turn or stop. But I was in luck: There was fresh powdery snow on the ground, which meant I kind of floated down the mountain. Though the others were already far ahead, carving in and out of trees, I could still see the tracks they left. Not knowing how to carve right off the bat, I'd go maybe 40 feet, then fall, then another 40 feet, then fall again. But every time, I got right back up, and trying to stay in their tracks actually helped me learn how to use my ankles and feet to shift my weight back and forth and to carve, heel to toe.

The fact that I'd played around on the skateboard helped me with snowboarding: I understood how to balance on a board. And because I'd skied all those years with my parents, I already knew how to move in the snow. So on my own, I made my way down the mountain, keeping my body flexible. As I rode, there was something so magical about the stillness of nature. The whistle of the wind through the trees. The serenity of the fresh-fallen snow. The sun glistening on the powder. The strength of my body as I used it to carve down the hill. By the end of the weekend, I was carving down the mountain in a kind of natural rhythm, going with the flow of the terrain. In a way, I felt like I was one with the board and in tune with the mountain itself.

It took about fifteen minutes for my friends to get to the bottom of the mountain. On that first try, it took me about thirty-five. As the sun set over the mountain that evening, I was wiped and a little bruised—but I couldn't have been happier. "Did you like it?" asked Aaron. "Heck yah!" I said. I'm sure the grin on my face had already given that away. Back then, snowboarding was pretty much a guy's sport, and there I was, almost keeping up with the boys. It felt awesome. We stayed to snowboard another day before we all piled back into the Bronco and headed home toward Vegas.

Sparks did fly with Richard and me. After that trip, he and I ended up snowboarding almost every weekend in Lee Canyon,

Nevada. The friendship lasted but the romance didn't. I broke up with him after just a month. That may have been a bad idea, because as soon as I called it quits, every other girl seemed to want him! But my love affair with snowboarding continued: It was love at first carve. I was hooked. Not just for the remainder of that season—but forever. There are no rules with snowboarding: It's just you on a board, using your imagination, riding off fallen-over trees and creating fun little tricks. It feels like freedom—freedom to play and do your own thing.

Even after Richard and I broke up, I still went snowboarding with the guys nearly every weekend. Cimarron had an early school day—we were in by seven, out by one—so a second after the final bell, we rushed home to get our gear and drive out of town. We didn't always have to drive all the way to Brian Head to get time on the slopes. There's a local resort called Ski Lee in Lee Canyon, and it's only a forty-five-minute drive from Vegas. On most of our trips, it was just me, my guy friends, and a big group of their snow-boarding friends. I was in heaven. By the time I was in high school, Mom had stopped making our lunches, so she instead gave us five dollars a day, and I would put the five bucks in my top drawer and save it to buy a twenty-five-dollar lift pass at the end of the week. I lived to snowboard.

When I started snowboarding, it wasn't just something I did. It became who I *was*. At a time when I was trying to figure out my place in the crazy world of high school, snowboarding helped me find my way and, in the end, myself. Even my style took shape: Yes, I still wore thrift store clothes and Vans, but my outfits were always put together tastefully and creatively. And from time to time, especially when I became a junior, I occasionally wore dresses and heels; I also loved doing my hair and makeup. No longer was I just Crystal Purdy's little sister. I was me—as free to create my own path as I was to make trails in the snow.

"WHAT DO YOU girls want to do after high school?" Dad asked. For dinner around the table that night, it was the four of us—me, Crystal, Dad, and Mom. My sister, then a senior, was a few months away from graduation; I was a sophomore. My father, who'd made his famous chicken wings that evening, was in the mood to talk about the future.

"I'm still thinking about what I want to do," said Crystal. "Maybe interior design." Like me, Crystal had worked for Uncle Rich's architectural firm, and during her time there, she got inspired to look into interior design.

My parents never pushed us to go to college, maybe because they hadn't gone themselves. Whether we wanted to go to trade school or college was totally fine with them, as long as we found a way to earn a living. They knew we'd figure out what we wanted. "Well, whatever you'd like to do," said Dad, picking up his third chicken wing, "we'll support you. Just make sure you can pay your car insurance and credit card bills." Crystal and I had credit cards in high school because my parents wanted to teach us to manage credit. One of the greatest lessons of my childhood was how to be smart with money.

I wasn't sure exactly what I would do after high school, but I did know that working at a bank or clothing store in a strip mall, as some of my classmates were planning, would feel like slow suicide for me. And besides that, I just had this intuition that something major was going to happen in my life. I didn't know where that feeling came from—but the closer I got to graduation, the less I could dismiss the hunch.

One evening on our back porch, my friend Beth and I got into a conversation about our plans. "I feel like I am destined to do so much more than stay in Vegas and work a normal job," I said. "Me, too!" Beth said. "Maybe I'll move to L.A. and try to break into acting." I nodded. I'd thought about acting as well, and I always had this desire to express myself, so moving to Los Angeles sounded like a great idea. And if she went to California, I might be able to go out there with her. Our conversation that night has always stayed with me. We both knew there were bigger things for us to do and we wanted to discover them.

The summer after her senior year, Crystal did decide to get into interior design—so she went down to a local school and signed up for a program. But by the second semester of my senior year at Cimarron, I was still thinking through my options. Beth began training as a massage therapist so she could earn some money while figuring out how to get into acting.

One evening, Beth invited me over to her place for a massage. She needed to practice her new skills on someone. Before I arrived, she set up the whole scene: candles, relaxing music, a table, the works. As she worked on my back, we chatted.

"What kind of things do they teach you in massage school?" I asked.

"All kinds of things," she said, pressing her fingertips down into my upper back. "Like this week," she continued, "I've been learning all about how the energy we carry in our bodies can create tightness in our backs."

"What are you going to do after your program's finished?"

"With all the cash I'll be making," she said, "I might be able to go ahead and move out to Los Angeles."

Around that time, I had two major lightbulb moments, and this conversation with Beth led to my first one. *What if I could train to be a massage therapist and then save up enough money to travel the world and snowboard?* Bingo.

My second *aha* moment came a few weeks before my graduation. My parents and I went up to Brian Head for the weekend. We stopped for dinner at a small restaurant near the resort. A waitress came to take our order. She was earthy: long, brown wavy hair, naturally gorgeous skin even without makeup, and maybe a few years older than me. She seemed so friendly that Mom struck up a conversation.

"Do you live up here?" Mom asked.

She nodded. "Yes," she said, "I'm from Vegas, but I've been up here with my dog and boyfriend snowboarding and working for a couple of years. But I just signed up for massage school. What I really want to do is travel, and I figure massage is a career I can take anywhere." I put down my menu and looked directly at her. All you have to do is say the word *travel* and you have my full attention.

"Where is the massage school?" Mom asked.

"It's over in Salt Lake City," she said.

"When do you go?"

"In a couple of months. I just need to find a roommate first." She then took our order and collected our menus. "I'm Charlet, by the way," she said, smiling again. "It's great to meet you." With that, she dashed off to the kitchen.

If you're fortunate in life, you have at least one moment when you know exactly what you should do. For me, this was that moment. "Hey, I know!" I blurted out to my parents. "I could move to Salt Lake and be that girl's roommate!" My parents stared at me for a long moment, probably because of how suddenly I'd made my decision. But when you know, you know, and I knew *instantly*.

Because of all those talks with Beth, I already had an idea of what it would be like to be a massage therapist, and heading off to Utah would at last get me out of Nevada. By the time we left the restaurant, Charlet had not only become my new best friend. She'd also become my future roommate. Done and done.

Within a week, I'd read up on the Utah College of Massage Therapy and signed myself up to start classes in June. I talked another friend of mine, Bryson, into moving from Vegas to Salt Lake. He had family there, and he wanted to work in their construction business. "You can even share a place with me and Charlet," I promised Bryson. So he made plans to pack himself up and meet us there.

On June 4, 1998, I graduated from high school. On the last page of my senior yearbook, there was a place for parents to write in a note to their children. My mother filled in a special message for me. "To Amy, our butterfly," she wrote. "You have grown into a beautiful young lady, inside and out. It's time to spread your wings and fulfill those dreams. Take our love and prayers with you and have lots and love of fun." I cried as I read it.

The next day, my dad packed all of my belongings in his truck, and my parents drove alongside me for the seven hours it took to get to Salt Lake. As we cruised along Interstate 15 North, all I could think about was how the world was completely open to me. Finally. Was I nervous? Maybe a little, because I didn't know what my new life would bring. But more than anything, I felt strong. Brave. Independent. Free. And ready to take on whatever I'd find on the other side of the horizon.

CHAPTER 4

A Different World

"What you love is a sign from your higher self of what you are to do."

—SANAYA ROMAN

The room reeked of formaldehyde. "Oh my gosh," one of my classmates whispered to me, tilting her head in the direction of a center table, "look at *that*." Along with fifteen other students at the Utah College of Massage Therapy, we'd gathered in a lab for a required course—anatomy. Just as I was about to respond, our professor cleared his throat. "Students," he said in a booming voice, "this is a female cadaver." Whoa.

The lifeless body of a woman lay stretched across the table. Her face and chest were covered with a sheet; her body had been drained of its blood. Her inner thigh was sliced open from her groin down to her knee, revealing every layer of fat, tissue, and muscle underneath her pale white skin. One of my classmates pulled the top edge of her T-shirt up over her mouth and nose and gagged. "If you're feeling sick," said our teacher, "you can step outside anytime and get some fresh air." Right then, two people ducked out of a nearby door.

You'd think I would've been grossed out. I wasn't. You don't sign up for a massage program that has one of the best anatomy courses in the country and then expect *not* to see a dead body. To truly understand the human form, you have to study its parts, and not just in a textbook. "I wonder how she died," I said to my friend. We'd never know. As I stared at her corpse, I found it fascinating that the only difference between a body that was alive and one that was dead is that the life force and spirit had exited.

That anatomy course was just a small part of my training. For six months, I threw myself into all kinds of coursework: Kinesiology. Yoga. Tai chi. Sports. Russian, and Swedish massage. Acupressure. Energy healing. Chinese medicine. Some of massage has its roots in Eastern philosophy, so our program was as much focused on the spiritual as it was on the physical—in other words, we did a lot of deep breathing and meditation. Each time I practiced what I was learning, I felt like I was connecting to an energy much bigger than my own. I loved it.

At the end of each school day, I drove the baby blue Toyota pickup I'd gotten by then to the home I shared with Charlet and Bryson. Our neighborhood was adorable: A winding road led up to our 1920s brick house, which was perched on a little hill just in front of a big mountain. Apricot trees dotted our street. In the fall, leaves of brown, gold, and red covered the lawns. The whole area looked vintage and historic. The truth is, I thought the neighborhood was charming simply because it was different from my hometown—flat Vegas is laid out on a grid. All it took was a winding road and a hill for me to get excited.

As much as I loved my new life, I did fly back to Vegas to visit. It felt nice to be back. After I settled in, hugged everyone, and caught up on my family news, we all sat around chatting on the back porch with some wine.

"I just heard the most terrible news," Mom said.

"Really?" I said, suddenly wondering if my mother was okay. Crystal and I exchanged a worried look.

"Well," Mom continued, "one of my friends' neighbors has a son who's really sick."

"What's wrong with him?" I asked, pulling my knees up to my chest.

"He contracted some kind of rare infection," Mom said. "The doctors had to amputate both his legs."

"Whoa," I said. "How old is he?"

"Well, that's the most heartbreaking part of it all," Mom said. "He's only nineteen."

"Holy cow," I said. I sat silent for a moment just to let that sink in. "Well, if something like that ever happened to me," I finally said, "you'd better get me to the nearest bridge as quickly as possible, because I'm going over. I'd never be able to handle anything like that." We shook our heads.

Later that evening, as I sat in the bathtub, shaving my legs, I thought, *What if I suddenly lost my legs? What would my life be like? How would I go on?* Frankly, the whole ordeal sounded like the kind of thing that happened to other people, people on *Oprah* or *Dateline NBC*. A few minutes later, I stood up and stepped out of the tub, and I seldom thought of the conversation again.

• • •

SCHOOL GOT MORE interesting by the course, and after learning so much about the philosophy of massage, I couldn't wait to get to work on an actual body. We warmed up slowly: For a couple of months in class, the other students and I practiced by massaging each other's backs; later, we moved to full-body massages. So by the time I took on my first few clients at the series of Sunday clinics the school set up for us, I was ready. Sorta.

The line was out the door at our first Sunday clinic. The school had advertised massages at, like, thirty dollars an hour for the general public. In other words, dirt cheap. When I arrived and scanned the line, I spotted every type of body: Skinny. Overweight. Tall. Short. Male. Female. Bald. Round. Athletic. I walked into my "room," a space separated from the other rooms by only a hanging sheet. I prepared my table.

My first client was a stocky middle-aged guy with dark brown hair. We greeted each other. "Just make yourself comfortable," I said, smiling nervously. "You can lie on your stomach—I'll start you facedown." He nodded, and I left so he could undress. To my surprise, when I returned a few minutes later, I found Chewbacca on my table! I have never seen a back so hairy. Seriously.

I tried not to gasp and went right to work. First, I rolled up a towel and put it under his ankles to create some lower-back support. Check. Next, I began gently kneading my fingertips into his back. Check. Then about halfway through the massage, I asked him to turn over. He did, and I began massaging his feet. After he'd been on his back for about ten minutes, something . . . popped . . . up. I could tell he was embarrassed because he tried to reposition himself. That's when my training kicked in: I suddenly began karate-chopping his thighs! That did the trick:

Within thirty seconds, all the excitement had died down. Literally.

Over the next few months of Sundays and beyond, I encountered every awkward situation you can imagine. Snoring. Crying. Laughing. And—how shall I put this?—a never-ending series of too much information. "My wife doesn't know this," one guy told me, "but I've been having an affair with our neighbor for seven months." I wasn't judgmental. Getting a massage is a way of releasing, and some people had a lot to release. Any great therapist can handle that, and I did.

By November 1998, I was done with the program. So was Charlet—and she moved back to Vegas to be closer to her boyfriend. A month after that, Bryson moved in with his family so he could save up some money. Most of the friends I'd made while in the program dispersed to places like Oregon and California so they could start their careers. That left me—a girl with a massage certification and an expiring lease.

I wasn't ready to leave Salt Lake. So I moved into a beautiful attic apartment with my new roommate, this hippie guy who owned every single cassette tape of the Grateful Dead. He lived upstairs in this huge house, and I had my own beautiful part of the attic; one of my massage school classmates—the one who'd told me about the opening—lived downstairs. This guy and I agreed that I could pay him a hundred bucks a month, and that the rest of my "rent" would be covered by giving him weekly massages. Deal. Unless I was working out the knots in the man's back, I never saw him.

Summer. Fall. Winter. By the start of 1999, I'd already experienced three seasons in Salt Lake. That February, my work came to an end, and I didn't yet have any leads on another steady job. Most of my friends had long since left Salt Lake, even the girl who'd lived in the big house with me and the hippie. And suddenly, around March, I started to realize something: All. My. Days. Seemed. Predictable.

So one Saturday morning that spring, I purposely woke up without a plan. I would just go with the flow of the day and see where it carried me. First, I hit the gym. I spent two hours on the treadmill, running to the Beastie Boys. Once back home, I did every single piece of my laundry I could find. Next, I went to get a vanilla latte at the coffee shop a few blocks away, and while out, I wandered over to a rock-climbing gym. *Maybe I'll spot a couple of cute guys.* I didn't—so I turned around and went back to the house. Inside, I flopped down on my bed and stared up at the ceiling. As I lay there, it hit me like a flying snowball to the back of the head: *I am bored.*

I had no one to talk to. I'm sure my hippie housemate was off somewhere zoning out to the Grateful Dead, so even he wasn't going to be any company. I had done absolutely everything I could do in a day in Salt Lake—and it was still only seven o'clock! At that point, I went into the living room and tried to turn on the TV. It didn't work. And that's when that flying snowball turned into an *aha* avalanche: *I've gotta get the heck out of here.*

Right then, I went into my room and started packing. Once I'd gathered all my stuff, I backed up my Toyota into the driveway so that it was as close as possible to the back door. I then put my possessions (all seven of them!) into the trunk. I carefully picked up my plant—the fifteen-foot ivy I'd been growing for months—and put it into the front passenger seat. I even managed to get my small pieces of furniture into the back of the truck. After everything was loaded, I left a hundred-dollar bill on the counter for the hippie (and no—I didn't leave a note) and then I jumped into the driver's seat and sped toward the highway. My destination? Brian Head. My parents had told me they'd be there for the weekend.

Nearly four and a half hours later, I knocked at the front door of my parents' condo. It was after midnight. "Who is it?" Mom called out. "It's me—Amy," I answered. Long pause. When she opened the door in her bathrobe, there I stood, holding only my ivy plant and my toothbrush. "Hon," she said, rubbing the sleep from her eyes, "what in the world are you doing here?" Without missing a beat, I made my declaration: "I'm coming home!"

My parents were in utter disbelief, and frankly, I was even more surprised than they were. Why did I want to go home so suddenly? Because I was homesick. My only "friend" was an ivy plant. I hadn't talked to anyone in town for days. My friends had moved on with their lives and moved to places like Portland and California. The whole situation was pitiful. And just like that—snap!—I realized I was over Salt Lake City.

As we pulled onto the long dirt road leading up to my parents' house, I knew I wouldn't stay in Vegas long. I was already sorting out my plans in my head: I could work for a year. Do some freelance massage. Save up cash. Move to a ski town and snowboard. Then maybe take off to Tahoe—or else get a job on a cruise ship. That's what's so cool about massage: It's portable. I could work in Europe, Africa, Asia. On a cruise ship, on an island, or in a resort town. All I needed was my hands and my massage table.

AFTER MY FRIEND Shane left Utah, he landed a big job in Vegas: He was hired as a manager at one of the most respected spas in the world, Canyon Ranch SpaClub. The spa was to open its doors in the enormous and luxurious Venetian hotel—and Shane was brought on to oversee the massage therapy team. I got back to Vegas right around the time he was staffing up. "You should apply here, Amy," he called me up to say. It was an honor to be asked to apply, because Canyon Ranch is not just any spa—it attracts the most talented therapists in the world. A few days after giving an amazing massage to one of the managers as part of the interview process, I landed the job.

I was already in career heaven, and my time at Canyon Ranch took me to a new level of paradise. I worked there in the mornings— four clients, back-to-back. Then in the afternoons, I worked as a therapist at Angel's Touch, a small day spa in town. As it turned out, Steve Wynn—the powerhouse businessman who oversaw much of the expansion of the Strip, including the Bellagio and the Mirage—had contracted with Angel's Touch to provide in-room massage services at some of his properties. I was asked to be one of the therapists to go out on calls.

I took the job, and from then on, I worked around the clock: mornings at Canyon Ranch, followed by being on call for in-room massages at the Bellagio and the Mirage between, say, 3 P.M. and 7 A.M. As if that weren't quite enough to keep me busy, I also took on any private clients I could manage to fit in. As hectic as my schedule was, my work was a thrill. Really.

A whole new world opened to me. I met the most interesting people from all over the globe: Australia, China, France, Brazil, South Africa, United Arab Emirates, I quickly moved my way up to do work in the villas—large, lavish private rooms at the Bellagio. Steve Wynn's personal guests were often booked in the villas.

And if you stayed in the villa, you had big money—and big stories to go along with that money. I regularly had high rollers on my table: celebrities, musicians, actresses, major businessmen. Any client could request a therapeutic massage. I began making more money than I ever had. At the Bellagio, I could earn $130 an hour, plus tips.

Happy and independent—that's how I felt during this time. I loved my flexible schedule. I loved the healing arts. I loved the amount of money I could make. And even though I'd never imagined I'd be back in Vegas, I also loved being close to my family. Crystal was living at home, too, and she was building her interior design business; she and her high school sweetheart—she'd been the head cheerleader, he'd been the top football player!—were engaged. They were planning a fall wedding. And my parents, of course, still had their hands in several businesses. We were four adults, living separate lives, and yet sharing our worlds with one another. I knew I'd leave Vegas eventually, but because I'd become more content than I ever thought I could be in my hometown, I was no longer in a huge rush.

One evening after I'd been home for about four months, Mom and I sat out on our back porch and chatted. As we talked, the sun descended over the valley and disappeared. "I feel so healthy and strong, so in control of my life," I told her. "And I'm making all this money! I feel like I'm on top of the world." And I did.

The next morning, I threw on my khakis and polo shirt and drove over to Canyon Ranch. "Can I put you down for a full day?" my manager, Shane, had asked me the day before. The busy summer travel season was under way, and he needed me to help with the influx of clients. "Sure," I said, "I'll be there." Around 9 A.M., I started my first massage; by 5 P.M., I'd finished my seventh. Just as I got to the parking garage, feeling relieved that it was time to go out with my friend Rob, Shane called me back to do that one last massage. That's when I met the old man. Little has been the same since.

CHAPTER 5

The Edge

"Life changes in the instant—the ordinary instant."
—JOAN DIDION

My shoulders felt achy. Normally, I could do several massages in a row at Canyon Ranch, go to the gym for a couple of hours, and still have plenty of energy left over for the Bellagio. But on one Thursday in July 1999, I was wiped. When I got to my third client, it took so much energy to massage him. I kept thinking, *Man, this guy is draining me!*

I left work early. The second I got home, I put on a white tank and crawled into the one place I've always escaped to when I'm sick—my parents' cozy king-size bed. They had a TV in their room, which meant I could at least watch while I lay there. Mom took my temperature. It was 101. "You don't look so good, honey," she said. I shrugged, sank my head deeper into the pillows, and dozed off.

It must be a twenty-four-hour bug, I thought. *I can probably just sleep it off.* The following morning, Friday, my whole family was planning to leave town for an event. Dad had started running these big Harley-Davidson motorcycle rallies, and there was one scheduled in Brian Head that weekend. "You should stay here and rest," said Mom. "Maybe you can come up later if you're feeling better." I wanted to go. The rallies felt like huge reunions, since my whole extended family would be up there. But by the next day, I still felt like crap.

"I hate leaving you," my mother said as she got ready that Friday morning. It was only seven o'clock—and she was heading off for some early appointments before swinging back home to pick up Crystal and then going to Brian Head. Dad had already driven up. "Mom, don't worry about it," I groaned. "I'm sure I'll be fine. As soon as I feel better, I'll just meet you guys there." A friend was driving up that afternoon—so I was planning to just ride up with him. As reluctant as my sister and mom were to go ahead without me, I reassured them I'd soon be feeling better.

I wasn't. Over the next two hours, I became sicker and sicker. Around noon, I made my way from my parents' bed and into the bathroom and threw up. From the road, Mom called to check on me. "How are you?" she asked. I went, "Aagh! I feel like I'm dying," which is pretty much how you do feel when you have the flu. "Try to drink some water," Mom said, sounding concerned—but probably reminding herself of my tendency to be dramatic. "I'm sure you're dehydrated. And if you feel like you need to go to the hospital, then go. I'll send your cousin over there to check on you." Michelle and Aunt Cindy had been the only family members who hadn't gone up to Brian Head. Back in bed, I wrapped myself tightly in a bunch of blankets and tried to make myself comfortable. About an hour or so after closing my eyes, I felt the need to wake up, but when I tried to open my eyes, I couldn't. Over and over I tried, but the exhaustion overtook me. I fell into a deep sleep.

Out of nowhere, I heard a sound. My eyelids shot open. "Amy, get up and look in the mirror," this voice said. *Who is talking?* Startled, I sat up in my bed. "Amy," I heard again, "get up and look in the mirror." *Is someone in the room with me?* The words sounded like a mix between a voice and my thoughts. As soon as I sat up, I realized something was really wrong. I had zero strength, my heart was beating out of my chest, and I was dizzy. When I stood, I couldn't feel my feet; they were numb, that feeling you have when a body part falls asleep. In the dusk light, I glanced down at my feet. They were purple. *Oh my God.* I then looked at my hands, and the same thing: purple. I looked in a mirror near the bed. What I saw still frightens me.

My nose, my chin, my ears, my cheeks—all pale purple. I panicked. My whole body shook, I broke into a cold sweat, and my heart began beating out of my chest. I felt sicker than I've ever felt. A second later, I heard footsteps. Michelle rounded the corner into my parents' room. "It's me," she said—and then she saw me. "Oh my God, Amy, you look dead!" she said. She dropped her purse and ran to me.

At the time, Michelle was only sixteen—so you can imagine how overwhelmed she felt. "We've gotta get you to the hospital!" she yelled. As I stumbled down the hall, I couldn't feel my feet—so my flip-flops flew in every direction. On my way out, I grabbed a jug of water. I had never been so thirsty. "We need to get out of here right now," I slurred. "Get your car."

Clearly, I was in no state to drive—so thank goodness Michelle had recently gotten her license. But just as we'd made it out the front door, she said, "Oh my God, Amy—I don't think I have enough gas!" I could barely even hold my head up.

"Then let's take my truck!" I told her.

"But I don't know how to drive a stick!"

"Well I'll *teach* you how to drive a stick right now!" I said in desperation.

We took Michelle's car. I figured that if she ran out of gas, we could call 911, which is what we should've done before we even left my house, but panic can make you forget everything you know. "Let's just go," I ordered. So she floored it through the desert while I curled my body up in a ball in the passenger seat. I had to stay alert enough to direct Michelle—we had a new hospital, and she didn't know where it was. The whole way there, I gasped for air. *Amy, just breathe,* I kept repeating in my head—but I couldn't seem to catch my breath. "Turn . . . *gasp* . . . right . . . *gasp* . . . here," I managed to say. She did—and her gas tank indicator inched closer to empty.

Fifteen minutes later, Michelle sped through the hospital parking lot and screeched right up to the sliding doors of the emergency room. She helped me out of the car and I fell to the ground. A passerby who'd spotted us getting out of the car rushed a wheelchair over to me. "Here you go, Miss, use this," he said. I was so frail that he had to lift me into the seat.

The ER was packed that evening. A long line stretched up to the front window. We checked in, and forty-five minutes later, a nurse finally wheeled me into the back, and then hoisted me up onto the table. All I wanted to do was lie down—and I tried to.

"I'm gonna need you to sit up," she ordered. She then Velcro'd a cuff around my left arm and took my blood pressure. She sat still for a few seconds and listened through the stethoscope. Then suddenly, she bolted from the room. "I need a doctor!" she screamed as she sprinted down the hall. Seconds later, a doctor and nurse rushed in and wheeled me away on a gurney.

My veins and lungs had collapsed. My blood pressure had crashed to a dangerously low level. My temperature was 103.5. In the intensive care unit, the doctor and nurse shouted over one another, trying to figure out what was happening to me. This nurse, a sweet redhead named Penny, poked around in my veins so she could hook me up to an IV—but she couldn't find my vein. My body was so numb that I, someone who has been terrified of needles since I was a kid, couldn't even feel the needle she was trying to stick in my arm. "Why can't I find a vein!?" she shouted at the doctor. "Because she's in cardiac arrest!" he yelled. *What? I'm in cardiac arrest?*

"Where are your parents, sweetie?" Penny pressed. My brain was foggy. "They're not here," I muttered. "They're out of town." Right then, the nurse grabbed the receiver of a bedside phone, one of those old-school beige phones with the long, windy cord. She gave me the receiver. I dialed my mom's number and handed the receiver back to her—given the state I was in, I'm surprised I was even able to dial. "Hello, Miss Purdy?" she said. Long pause. "Your daughter is in the Mountain View emergency room. We have no idea exactly what's wrong with her, but you need to get here as fast as you can; her entire body is crashing and at this rate she has maybe two hours left to live." Click.

Right then, frightened to death, the words the old man told me began reeling through my head: "Don't be scared. Don't be scared. Don't be scared." While the medical team shouted across me, all I could do was picture the wrinkly face and dark skin of that man who'd told me he'd crossed over. "I think the same thing is going to happen to you one day," he whispered, "and when it does happen, don't be scared." *Was this my time? Was I crossing over? And what did that mean?* Whatever it meant, I clung to his words. I then passed out.

My eyes reopened around four the next morning. I was hooked up to a dialysis machine, with IVs all around me. My mom, sister, and aunt were standing in a half circle around my bed. My mom, who had broken every speed limit to get there from Brian Head, making the trip in two and a half hours, had my sister with her. Dad, who'd had to quickly arrange for his partner to oversee the remainder of the Harley event, was on his way.

At first, my family didn't say anything, but I could read the shock and worry on their faces. Before we could exchange a word, Dr. Abby, a Sri Lankan ER surgeon with rich brown skin and kind eyes, pulled Mom aside. Dr. Nowins, my primary care physician, was with him. "Your daughter's in severe septic shock," Dr. Abby explained. "Her kidneys are completely shut down. In all my years of practice, I've never seen anyone pull out of massive kidney failure as bad as this." When Mom responded, her voice quivered: "Are you saying that Amy could die?" Dr. Abby nodded. "We don't know exactly what's causing this," he said, "but we do know that her white blood count is over one hundred thousand—and that indicates a massive blood infection." Dr. Nowins chimed in. "She has maybe less than a two percent chance of surviving."

By the time Dad got there at 4:30 A.M., I was in grave condition.

If I lifted my arm, jerked my hand, or shifted my body in even the tiniest way, all the machines I was hooked up to would start beeping like crazy. The doctors were already filling me with fifty gallons of saline to keep pressure in my collapsed veins. Over the next twenty-four hours, I'd go from 125 to 175 pounds from the weight of the saline. When my dad arrived, I could tell from the look on his face that he was stunned by the state I was in. "Oh, sweetheart," my father said, leaning over to kiss my forehead. "Dad's here—and I'm not going to leave your side." A warm tear rolled from my lower lid and onto my cheek.

After Dr. Abby had gone, my mom came and stood at the side of my bed with my dad. "Mom, what have I gotten myself into here?" I whispered. She could barely make out my words because my breathing had become so labored. Mom stroked my hair away from my face. "Honey," she said, stifling her own tears, "I don't think you've gotten yourself into anything. The question is what's gotten into you."

SEPTIC SHOCK—THAT'S WHAT happens when the body pulls blood from your extremities to save your organs. When I was admitted, no one quite knew what was making me so sick. Because my blood pressure was so low, the doctors thought I was in heart failure. I wasn't. Next, they thought I had toxic shock syndrome. But after some tests, they also ruled out TSS. Finally, due to my elevated white blood count, they concluded that I had a serious blood infection—they just didn't know what kind. That's why they'd sent my blood to be cultured. It would take five days to get the results.

Miraculously, I made it through the rest of the night. Dr. Abby, who'd been monitoring my condition even after he'd left the hospital, returned to my room with some news. "We're going to need to put Amy into a medically induced coma," he said. Dad wrinkled his brow. "Really?" he said. "Yes," said the doctor. "While we're awaiting the cultures, we need to keep her system stable—that's the only way we can keep her major organs from failing." Meanwhile, I was gasping for every bit of oxygen I could get. Can you imagine what it feels like to have your head pushed underwater with no certainty that you'll get your next breath? That's the major discomfort I felt. In addition, I had zero kidney function; that's why I'd been put on 24/7 dialysis.

Tears welled up in my dad's eyes as he signed the consent forms to hand my life over to the medical team and put me fully on machines. "Can I see my feet?" I murmured to my dad after he was done signing. "Sweetie, the last thing we're worried about is your feet," he said. "I know," I said, "but—*gasp*—they're—*gasp*—so—*gasp* cold," I whispered. After I complained a few more times, my dad walked down to the foot of my bed. He lifted the white sheet and took off my socks. If my feet were purple before, they were an intense violet at this point. A few inches above my ankle was the line of demarcation—pale white skin above, purple skin below. I wept when I saw them. Dad pulled the sheet back over onto my feet and squeezed my hand. "We're going to get through this, sweetie pie."

The anesthesiologist arrived to put me in a coma. The last thing I remember was being surrounded by a roomful of family and friends, all wearing protective yellow masks and gowns and latex gloves; until my diagnosis could be confirmed, the doctors had to protect anyone who entered my room. The CEO of the hospital, a Mormon and a friend of my sister, placed his hand on my forehead and prayed. "God our Heavenly Father," he said, "I pray that you take care of our dear Amy, that she may survive, and that she will walk on this earth on her own two feet again"—and then I was out.

Once I was under, Dr. Abby left. But forty minutes later he had a sudden strong feeling that he needed to head back to the hospital and do something more to save me. He had no idea how he was going to do that, but he formulated a plan as he drove. Under the surgeon's new direction, the nurses spent an entire day slowly transferring me from my bed to the CAT-scan bed. Any abrupt movement would've made my blood pressure fall and my heart rate shoot up. When they finally did move me, my blood sugar crashed dramatically, and luckily, they were able to stabilize it. Good thing Dr. Abby followed his intuition: The scan showed that my spleen was ten times its normal size! So Dr. Abby rushed me into the operating room and performed emergency surgery. My spleen had indeed burst—and he got it out in just enough time to save my life.

Somehow, even in a coma and under intense anesthesia, I was still conscious of certain sounds. I could hear the doctors and nurses talking to each other. Then at some point during the surgery, Dr. Abby uttered a sentence that will stay with me forever: "Whatever it is you believe in, Amy," he whispered, "think about that now." The first thought that came to my mind was *I believe in love.* I was still aware of sensations—like my heart pounding out of my chest. *Ba-boom. Ba-boom. Ba-boom.* And although I didn't feel any actual pain from it, I could sense the pressure of Dr. Abby slicing me open from my sternum down to my navel and my skin pulling apart. It felt as if I was somehow outside of myself, looking up at the doctors and nurses as they worked. I had no earthly emotion—nothing like fear. It was just a matter-of-fact awareness that I was in surgery.

My heart began racing at 226 beats per minute. "Code blue!" the doctor shouted. "We're losing her!" The entire medical team rushed in with a crash cart in an attempt to shock my heart back to a normal rhythm. As I lay there, I thought, *I know these doctors are trying to save me . . . but I'm going . . . I'm going . . . I'm going right now.* I was hanging on by my fingertips, and with each heartbeat, I slipped closer to the edge. Then all at once—GASP!—my heart pounded so hard it took my breath away. I felt as if I was being pulled away from my body. Everything went black. I found myself in a boundless dark space. I felt weightless, as if I was floating. There was no gravity. I wasn't aware of my physical body anymore. It was clear to me what had happened—I'd died.

I saw a light—not the kind of bright light you often hear of in stories of near-death experiences, but rather a foggy green tint that had been there when I entered the darkness. In this dim light, I saw the silhouettes of three figurines. Each was a different height. I couldn't make out any human characteristics, like skin, eyes, or hair. But they had enough of a human shape to them—a head, arms, and hands—that I recognized them as some kind of beings. I didn't have the feeling they were anyone I'd ever known.

The silhouettes were communicating to me, not in an audible voice, but as if their minds were speaking to my mind. I understood clearly what they were saying. "You can come with us," I heard, "or you can stay." They moved their arms to signal me toward them, and I suddenly felt extremely frustrated. I understood the choice I was being given—whether I wanted to live or die. With every bit of energy in me, I revolted: *I haven't even lived my life! And you're asking me whether I want to leave?!*

A split second later, a wave of earthly memories washed over me: The smell of rain. The sound of waves crashing on the beach. The metallic taste of hose water I drank as a kid. The feeling of powdery snow under my feet. The laughter of my mom, dad, sister, and cousins. All the sensory experiences I loved. "You can come with us, or you can stay," the beings again communicated. "But know that if you stay, you may not return to the life you lived before." I had just one thought: *If I go with you, I'll be leaving behind too much.* With every bit of energy in my being, I yelled, "No! I'm not going anywhere!"

Then in the pitch black, a bright white light appeared—a light different from the foggy one I'd seen before. This one was blindingly bright. It sat above my right shoulder, and it communicated a message to me: "You made the choice to return. You will have major challenges in your journey, and you will also experience great beauty. Just understand that no matter what happens in your life, it will all make sense in the end."

The whole space turned black. Then suddenly, my lungs filled with air—as if I'd gone from having no breath to being able to breathe fully. The air filled every part of my lungs. It was the deepest, most fulfilling breath I'd ever taken—and somehow, it felt like there was gratitude mixed in with the oxygen. There's only one way I can describe it: I call it the breath of life.

MY EYELIDS FLEW open. My vision was foggy. I was in a hospital room. I had no idea exactly how much time had passed or all that my body had gone through. My whole family stood around my bed. I tried to speak. "I . . . I had," I stuttered—but I couldn't get any words out of my mouth because I kept choking on the breathing tube. "What are you saying, sweetie?" my mom asked. The doctor tried to explain: "Patients sometimes move their mouths like they're speaking because they want the tube out of their throats," he told her. *No!* I thought. *I have something to say!* I tried to speak once more but still couldn't. Then I passed out again.

In the following days, I drifted in and out of consciousness. A couple of days after the spleen surgery, doctors slowly began taking me off the medicine they'd used to induce a coma, which is why I was in and out. While in a deep sleep, I had a vision that seemed as real to me as this page you're reading now. A curly-haired man came up alongside my bed and began talking to me. I don't recall everything we spoke about, but I will always recall the sentence he uttered as he turned to leave: "Just remember," he told me, "the only way is the shaman way." Though I still had the tube down my throat, I began repeating his words to myself. "The only way is the shaman way," I mouthed.

Meanwhile, as I lay there unconscious, my mother later told me that she rallied the prayer warriors. "I don't know what your religious beliefs are," she announced to all the dozens of friends who'd gathered in the waiting room, "but if you believe in prayer, now is the time to pray." Dr. Abby already had all of his family and friends in Sri Lanka praying. He also showed up daily to pray for me, and then place a dot of ash in between my eyes and forehead; when I awakened briefly, I always knew he'd been there because I could smell his cologne and feel the ash. Also, Dr. Nowins told my mom, "I'm pretty sure the whole world is praying for Amy." She had friends in her homeland of the Philippines praying for my healing, and I felt each and every one of those prayers. My parents opened the doors to anyone who wanted to pray over me—bishops, priests, pastors, spiritual teachers, no matter what religion they were. Even in my coma, it was as if I could hear these hundreds of whispers, each carrying a feeling of love.

Throughout this entire ordeal, some of my nurses became as emotionally and physically exhausted as my family and me. While I was in the coma, one nurse in particular watched over me as if I was her own daughter. She manually adjusted my machines around the clock in order to control my blood pressure and heart rate. That was such a stressful and tedious job that, at one point, the poor woman nearly fell apart—and thank goodness my aunt Debbie, a fellow nurse, was there to support her. "I can't do this anymore!" the nurse shouted through sobs. "It's okay, hon," my aunt consoled. "I know this is tough."

At last, I awakened, this time more fully. I looked around slowly. I had tubes coming out of every part of my body, and I was surrounded by IVs. I studied each of my family members' faces. My parents looked like they'd aged two decades. My mom, who was already petite, looked as if she'd dropped ten pounds. Crystal's long hair, usually flowing beautifully down her back, was pulled into a messy ponytail. None of my family had left the premises for days. My father slept at my side in a narrow, uncomfortable chair. My mom and sister had camped out in a little room that the hospital let them move into, Crock-Pot and all.

I glanced around the room and spotted some familiar items. One of my paintings hung on the wall. Photos of me with my friends were all around my bed. Candles and flowers filled the room. The Dave Matthews Band played softly in the background. While I was out, my mom and Crystal had raced home to gather all my favorite things—including a few of my CDs. They wanted to keep me connected to earth. My mom even had on my favorite necklace, the one with the snowflake pendant that she'd bought me for my sixteenth birthday.

"We're not going to let a single negative thought into this room," Mom had declared to all the friends and family who'd gathered. "We're going to surround Amy with love and positive energy." Mom knew how fragile I was—and that any outburst of grief or even a split-second mention of death could open the door for that to happen.

The first day when Aunt Debbie, the nurse, came by, she took one look at the machines and my stats in my medical charts and immediately realized how close to the edge my life dangled. "Oh my God!" she shouted. "Amy's dying!" That was enough to set off Grandma Campbell, who began wailing. "Stop!" my mom yelled. "There is no crying allowed in this room!" She ushered both of them out to the hall. "All it will take is the smallest negative thought or movement, and she may leave us."

When my eyelids did at last slide open again, my mother was standing by—ready to keep me conscious as long as she could. Again, I tried to speak. When she noticed me struggling, she darted out of the room. A minute later when she returned, she was holding a pencil and a sheet of paper. She handed both to me. Slowly taking the pencil with my weak hand, I scribbled a bunch of words, including *shaman*. On the lower part of the paper, I wrote out one full sentence as legibly as I could: "I had a choice— and I chose to live."

CHAPTER 6

Awake

> "We are not human beings having a spiritual experience.
> We are spiritual beings having a human experience."
> —PIERRE TEILHARD DE CHARDIN

My family had no idea what my note said—it might as well have been written in hieroglyphics. All they could make out were a couple of words I'd faintly scrawled: *shaman* and *choice*. My mom, who knew I was trying to communicate something about being on the brink of death, was encouraging. "We're here with you now, sweetie," she kept telling me. But because I still couldn't speak, I had no way to tell them what had actually happened—that I'd traveled to the doorway of death and chosen not to walk through it.

On the evening that I awakened and scrawled that note, I'd been in a coma for a week. But even after I became conscious and the doctors eased me off life support, I continued drifting in and out because the medication wasn't fully out of my system. In total,

I was in and out of consciousness for close to two weeks. And during the entire process, my parents were sitting on the edges of their seats. They'd been warned by the doctors that I might never wake up. In addition to organ failure, the medical team had discovered that I had disseminated intravascular coagulopathy (DIC)—which, for short, the nurses sometimes referred to as "death is coming." And at any moment, said doctors, a blood clot could go to my heart or brain. "You may want to prepare to say your goodbyes," Dr. Abby told my parents. "And if your daughter survives, she may have brain damage, paralysis, or hearing loss along with many other challenges." It is borderline miraculous that I ever even opened my eyes again.

By the time I did come out of the coma, I was still relying on my breathing tube for every breath. Yet in order for me to work my way off life support, I needed to slowly build up lung strength. So about a week after I awakened, the nurses withdrew my tube—and when they did, it felt as if my lungs were being ripped out of my chest. I began gasping for air. The nurses stayed by my side to make sure I was breathing okay. I wasn't. My lungs throbbed in pain and barely expanded. It's the scariest feeling to not be able to get a full breath, and the more I panicked, the harder it became.

A few hours after the nurses left the room, I was sure I was dying. With tears covering my face, I yelled, "Get—*gasp!*—the nurse—*gasp!*—Mom!" On a scale of 1 to 10, the pain in my chest was a 25. Out of everything I'd already been through, this experience was the first that truly scared me; now that I was awake, I became fully connected to my body and emotions for the first time. "Mom, I can't do it!" I cried. "Honey," she said, "you have no choice. You have to." She knew how frightened I was, and she hated to see me suffer, but the last thing she wanted was for the doctors to put me back on life support. As I continued weeping, she pushed the emergency alarm on my bed rail. Three nurses bolted in. They told me the same thing Mom had said: "We know it's uncomfortable, but if we put you back on the breathing tube, there's a chance you'll never come off."

Let me tell you, those were the two hardest days of my life. My parents had their hardest days early on, but for me, this was the first time I was awake and aware and truly frightened. I did eventually begin to breathe easier, and once I did, the condition of my kidneys improved ever so slightly. That's when doctors moved me from around-the-clock dialysis to once a day; I started to urinate on my own, and all that extra water weight began shedding. Every minute of every day, I felt the sickest you can feel. The nurses kept a pink plastic throw-up bucket right next to my bed, because I vomited up to seventeen times a day. Even though I felt like death, I did go from having less than a 2 percent chance of survival to a 15 percent shot.

Once the nurses finally pulled the tube out of my throat, I was more than ready to speak. "The only way is the shaman way," I whispered. I still didn't know what that meant, but I knew I didn't want to forget it. I told my mom about the man who visited me. "Yes, honey," she said, nodding as she stroked my hand. "Did a curly-haired man ever come here?" I asked. The answer was no, which confirmed that my visitor had indeed been a vision I'd had while I was unconscious.

The whole time I was in the coma, Dr. Abby stayed on a 24/7 detective hunt. Here's what's so amazing about Dr. Abby: After my spleen operation, he'd been assigned off my case and called away to do surgeries at other hospitals around Vegas. As an ER surgeon, he was in high demand. Yet every day, even if it was midnight or he was all the way across town, he came by to check on me and say a prayer. He wanted to know: What was this mysterious infection that was threatening the life of a nineteen-year-old?

Five days after I was admitted, he and the other doctors finally got an answer. "Your daughter has bacterial meningitis," Dr. Abby told my parents. He went on to explain that the condition, also known as meningococcal disease, is spread like the cold or flu. So if someone, say, sneezes on you in an elevator, you could be exposed. Many people are carriers—one in four people—but very few actually get sick with it. According to the National Meningitis Association, between 800 and 1,200 Americans contract the disease each year, and 20 percent of all cases occur in teens and young adults; of those who get sick with the blood infection, 10 to 15 percent die from it within the first twenty-four hours of the symptoms' onset; among the survivors, one in five live with permanent disabilities such as brain damage and loss of kidney function. Like most people, I'd heard of meningitis, but I never knew I was at risk.

When Dr. Abby first mentioned the word *meningitis,* my mom thought of the more widely known form of the disease—spinal meningitis, also know as viral meningitis. The U.S. Centers for Disease Control and Prevention has identified five types of meningitis, and viral meningitis is far more common—and usually far less deadly—than the kind I had. As little as my parents knew about bacterial meningitis, one thing was completely clear to them: I was on my deathbed. Upon hearing the diagnosis, my mom began weeping, while my dad, too stunned to even speak, stood by and rubbed her back. You can imagine how frustrated my parents were when, later in the elevator, a doctor not on my case said, "You know there's a vaccination for that, right?" "What?!" my mom yelled. "You mean this all could've been prevented?"

Meningitis is a horrible infection, and the kind I contracted is one of the worst. It can move extremely fast: Once the bacteria gets into your bloodstream, it shoots off thousands of toxins that double in number every twenty minutes. The signs of meningitis, which usually become noticeable a few days after exposure, are fever, stiff neck, chills, and vomiting. It appears a lot like the flu, which is partially why it's so deadly—many who come down with it don't at first recognize how sick they are. Another symptom is a purple rash all over the body, and that can start a day or two before the other symptoms take hold. In my case, that rash never appeared, so I had no reason to think I had anything other than the flu.

Even after my breathing tube was removed, the poking and prodding continued. Every day at 4 A.M., I woke up to the pinch of needles as a nurse drew my blood. Soon after that nurse had left, an X-ray technician would walk in and flip the lights back on. He'd grab my arm, pull me into an upright position, and slide an ice-cold metal tray behind my back so he could capture an image of my lungs. They didn't look good. The left one was filling with fluid, making it even harder for me to breathe. Just when I'd recovered from that X-ray, another nurse would come in and stick a four-inch, hollow-gauge needle into my back, in between my ribs, and through the muscle. "Let me know when you can feel this going into your lung," the nurse said. Once I gave her the sign, she then sucked out enough fluid to fill a two-liter soda bottle.

I didn't cry. When you're in crisis mode, you go into this "survive now, cry later" mind-set—and that's the mind-set I was in. There was this one day, however, when a nurse came to remove some tape from the left side of my back after a lung surgery (doctors had to operate to take out a portion of my left lung) and when she ripped off the tape, I screamed and broke down into tears. I'd been ripped on and poked so much that I couldn't take it one more time. I didn't want her or my parents feeling sorry for me, so I shouted, "Just so you all know, I'm not crying because I'm sad! I just don't want to be *touched* anymore!"

Awhile after I was awake and off the breathing tube, my former art teacher Miss Lyle came to visit. My mom told her what I'd said about the shaman. Miss Lyle, a very spiritual person, responded, "Oh my gosh, I know what a shaman is. It's a healer." She returned a few days later with several books on shamanism. My mom opened the first page of one of the books and read a few paragraphs aloud. "Shamans are healers," she read. "Many times, they have gone through a traumatic or life-altering event that leads them to become healers in their communities. Many shamans claim to have had near-death experiences. When they've returned to Earth, they often believe they've returned with the power to heal others." My mom and I looked at each other in disbelief. "That's what happened to me," I whispered. "Does this make me a shaman?" I had no idea. But I did know that I'd been visited by a man who encouraged me to take that path.

JOHN F. KENNEDY Jr. died in a plane crash on July 16, 1999—the same day my cousin rushed me to the ER. A few weeks later when I came out of the coma, that headline still dominated the news.

JFK Jr., his wife, Carolyn Bessette, and Carolyn's sister, Lauren, had been on their way from New Jersey to the wedding of John's cousin when their plane, which John was piloting, nosedived into the Atlantic off Martha's Vineyard. That news, along with the ordeal I was enduring, made me poignantly aware of how fragile our lives are. In the blink of an eye—in less time than it takes to inhale—everything can change. Everything.

Post-coma, I spent most of my time sleeping. When I was awake, I'd just lie there and watch the air from the fan blow across the hundreds of get-well cards taped to my walls. Each time the air passed, the cards fluttered like butterfly wings. As I watched, I couldn't stop thinking about the other world I'd been transported to. The peace and stillness of the black space. The message of the beings: "You can come with us, or you can stay." The reassurance I was given as I turned back: "It will all make sense in the end."

Had this been what the old man meant by "crossing over"? Had he been given the same choice to go or to stay? Had he encouraged me to not be scared because he knew something traumatic would happen to me, and how did he know? Was "crossing over" some kind of spiritual awakening? And if it was, how would my life be different? Why was I given a second chance? I didn't know whether I'd find any of the answers. I only knew that I'd make this second chance at life a meaningful one.

CHAPTER 7

Ground Shift

"A bend in the road is not an end in the road—
unless you fail to make the turn."

—HELEN KELLER

My legs were in trouble. From the minute I awakened from my coma, I saw that my feet were horribly swollen and discolored. The nurses came in daily and rubbed a special cream on my feet, hoping that would restore circulation. No doctor needed to get up and make an announcement like, "Attention, Amy: You may lose your feet." It was clear that I might lose my legs—and that the doctors were doing all they could to save them.

"Your feet look like a mummy's feet," Crystal joked one morning about five weeks after I'd been in the hospital. I smiled a little; as serious as my condition was, we all tried to keep a sense of humor. "I know, they are hideous," I groaned. Not only were they swollen, but the bottoms of them were black. To make it worse, I'd painted my toenails in this rich copper color just before I became ill. So the combination of copper polish against my charcoal-colored feet was very unflattering, as in straight out of a tomb from Egypt. "You should let me change your toenail polish," she insisted. An hour later, my toenails were bright red, and my sister, ever the fashionista, seemed pleased.

Around this time, I got another angel doctor: Dr. Canale. He was the sweetest man. He happened to be a friend of the family—he knew my aunt Debbie. "Hello, Amy!" Dr. Canale always cheerfully greeted me. He was tall with reddish round cheeks, grayish blond hair, and a compassionate smile. "Let's see how those legs are progressing." After he examined me, I asked him the same question I'd asked each of my doctors: "Will I ever be able to snowboard again?" "Well," said Dr. Canale, "we don't know, Amy. And to be honest with you, we don't even know whether you'll be able to walk without a cane, let alone snowboard, but we will do everything we can."

My heart sank. The idea that I'd never again feel the freedom of carving down a mountain was so overwhelming to me that I couldn't think about it for more than a second or two. "I'm going to do my best to set you up so that you can be as active as possible, whatever the outcome is," said Dr. Canale, trying to leave me with some hope. Every time I told my parents how much I wanted to snowboard again, my father always had the same answer: "Baby steps, sweetie. We need to first take care of your feet and get you walking."

The first several times we met, Dr. Canale didn't say much about amputation. "We're still doing everything we can to save your legs," he said. But a little at a time, we all realized my legs weren't improving. At last, Dr. Canale told my family what we'd already been discussing and fearing for weeks: "Your daughter may have to have her legs amputated." He held back tears as he said it—he'd wanted to believe as much as we all did that my legs would heal.

My parents stood quiet. Then my mom launched in with a whole list of questions, including some I wouldn't have even thought of. "Will she still be able to have children one day?" my mother asked. "And will she be able to swim with prosthetics? And if you do have to amputate her legs, how much of them can you save?" My father had his questions, too, some of them similar: "Can you just amputate her toes? Or how about just her feet—at the line of demarcation near her ankle bone?" "You don't want to do that," the surgeon told him. "We need to take off enough so she can fit prosthetics under her without her being too tall, yet leave enough so that she has leverage for the sports she loves, like snowboarding and wakeboarding." The best place to amputate, he explained, would be at around ten inches down my shin.

When something like this happens, it's easy to get into "what if" mode—and I struggled with whether I'd done something that could've caused my condition. *How did I even contract meningitis?* When I reflected on the weeks leading up to July 16, I went through every single day, every action I took. For instance, I ate some pineapple that tasted a little spoiled. Could that have been it? Or this: The weekend before I got sick, I went out to a lake and some hot springs with a few work friends. I cut my toe on a rock while climbing up a waterfall. *Could that cut have caused the infection?*

Here's what I know: You can spend your whole life questioning. You can scrutinize every little thing you said or did, every little decision you did or didn't make. It's normal to look back. We're human, so we want to understand things—and yes, sometimes there are lessons to be learned. But ultimately, it doesn't help to *keep* looking. Or regretting. Or berating yourself for what you can't go back and change. It's a waste of energy. In the hospital, I had a basic choice—to either gaze into the rearview mirror, or keep my eyes fixed on the road right in front of me. I chose the latter.

I LOVE THUNDERSTORMS. I always have. The smell of the rain reminds me of sitting on the back porch with my dad, looking out over the desert to see the clouds gather over the gleaming lights of Vegas. It's magical. "Dad?" I said at a little before midnight one evening while in my hospital bed; it was raining. My father had nodded off in his chair. My mom and Crystal had gone home just for that evening. Dad sat up when he heard my voice. "Yes, sweetie? What is it?" I looked over at him. "I wish I could go out and smell the rain," I said. "I miss it." My dad first shot me a look that said, "I don't think so," but then a moment later, a grin slowly spread across his face. "You know what," he said, "let's do it. Let's get you outside to smell the rain." He jumped up to his feet.

Now I've gotta tell you: From where I lay, that sounded pretty impossible. I'd been hooked up to machines for weeks. I was days away from potentially losing my legs. But none of that stopped my dad: He marched out to the front desk and got to work. "Excuse me," he said to one of the nurses. "My daughter wants to smell the rain. How can I get her outside?" The nurse looked at my father like he had six heads. "Well, sir," she said. "I'm not sure—"

"She just wants to smell the rain. We don't have to be out there for very long," he insisted. "She's not on life support anymore. And she has been holed up in this hospital since the middle of July."

Minutes later, two nurses were in my room, unhooking me from the walls and trying to figure out how to make me portable. Even just thinking about it now makes me want to cry. They found a way to wheel me out of the front doors of the hospital, the same doors my cousin had wheeled me into weeks before. I hadn't been outdoors since.

The nurses parked me on a sidewalk near the front edge of the parking lot. Thankfully, because it was so late, not many people or cars were around. They set me up as best as they could, IV and all, and elevated my bed by a couple of inches so I could see. They then left me and Dad to ourselves. They even brought out a chair for my father so he could sit comfortably next to my bed.

It was warm out, probably 90 degrees. The sky was seemingly infinite. The coming storm had turned it a gorgeous mix of blue, purple, and maroon. A gentle breeze brushed across my face and stirred my sheets. Way off in the distance, the thunder roared every half minute or so, as if to demand some kind of answer. I lay there and looked up in silence—just me and my dad.

I breathed in the fresh smell of the impending rain—slow, big breaths—and filled up my lungs each time. And as crazy as it might sound, given all that I'd gone through, in this moment I'd never been more grateful to be alive. Never more appreciative of having my father's love. Never more thankful to have been given a second chance. "Dad?" I finally said after about thirty minutes. He looked over at me, then reached for my hand and squeezed it tightly. "Yes, sweetie?" I paused, then looked directly at him.

"Thank you," I whispered. "Thank you so much." The pitter-patter of light rain hit the ground. The nurses returned to wheel me inside.

AS AMPUTATION SEEMED more and more likely, I tried to wrap my brain around the idea, and to be honest, I couldn't really grasp it. Some people lose their legs in an instant, like in a car crash, and they have no time to think about it. Others live with a debilitating illness, and they sometimes have months or years to fear an upcoming amputation. I felt like I was someplace in the middle. What would my life be like? Could I still be a massage therapist? Was Dr. Canale right that I might end up using a cane? And was there even a snowball's chance in hell that I would ever snowboard again?

The only person without legs I'd ever seen was a wounded soldier, sitting in a wheelchair wearing his fatigues and holding up a sign that read, "Vietnam vet: Will work for food." Beyond that, I had no frame of reference, no idea what it would actually be like to live with no legs. And besides that, I really couldn't let myself go there for more than a few minutes: Why break down over something when you're not yet 100 percent sure it'll happen?

My best anchor became the present moment. In order to get through everything, I just had to focus on getting through what was right in front of me. Even now, people often ask me, "Weren't you depressed when you realized you might lose your legs?" I wasn't at first—and some of my family and friends thought I was in denial. But I was just compartmentalizing in order to make it through each day. I didn't let myself slide into a dark spot, mostly because it didn't feel good for me to linger there. If I would've dug a hole and buried myself in it, I would have never come out. I couldn't have known it at the time, but my darkest moments weren't there in the hospital; they were still to come.

In a way, I was staying strong for my family. I could see the stress in their faces. They were all so heartbroken. Do you have any idea what it's like to stand by on the sidelines as someone you love faces serious trauma? Just ask my mom, my dad, Crystal, and the rest of my family. They can tell you that it's completely heart-wrenching. You feel helpless. So out of control. When I saw their anguish, it made me want to show them that I was going to be okay. That they didn't have to worry about me. Their heartache actually *fueled* me. It made me want to get the heck out of that hospital bed.

I was the one feeling sad for my loved ones, especially Crystal. There she was, right in the middle of planning her wedding, and then—bam—everything came to a halt for her and her fiancé, Jared. Her dress had been ordered, the guest list settled, the vendors booked, the money invested. The date was set for October 15. It was already mid-August, and we had no idea how much longer I'd be in the hospital. "Please don't worry about it, Amy," she kept saying, trying to reassure me. "If we have to push back the date, we will. I just want you to get better." I appreciated her sweetness and flexibility, but the truth is I felt sick about ruining the buildup to her big day.

But my legs just weren't getting better. And here's when I knew my doctors had moved me out of the "possible amputation" category and into the "almost inevitable" one: They set me up to meet a prosthetist who could introduce me to the whole new world of legs. Dr. Canale thought this guy would be a great prosthetist for me. He was young, spirited, and had himself lost a leg.

"Hello, Amy," the guy said once he rounded the corner into my room. "I'm Kevin." He was wearing khaki pants with a tucked-in polo shirt. He was in his early thirties and good-looking: muscular, a chiseled jaw, and long layers of dirty-blond hair. He walked in with a limp in his left leg; not a major one, but enough of a swing for me to notice. He offered me his hand.

"Hi," I said. We shook hands. "Nice to meet you." Kevin set down his bag and pulled up a chair next to my bed.

"Well, I'm sure you're wondering what to expect when it comes to prosthetics," he said. I nodded. All day, I'd been looking forward to meeting him; strangely, I was even excited, because I'd get a look into this whole new world that I knew nothing about. "Well," he said, "let me first tell you how I lost my leg. I got into a motorcycle accident a few years back. I ended up having to have my leg amputated above the knee."

"Oh really?" I said. I looked down toward his leg, but because he had on pants, I couldn't see his prosthetic.

"Yes," he said. "And right after I got the leg, there was definitely a period of adjustment."

"How is it now?" I asked.

"It just feels like part of my life."

I shook my head, then dove right into my burning question: "Do you think I can snowboard on prosthetic legs?"

He paused. "I've never seen a double-amputee snowboarder. But there are skiers."

"But I'm not a skier," I clarified. "I'm a snowboarder."

"Well, it's possible that you may be able to snowboard, but I've just never seen it."

He went on to tell me about the many different types of prosthetics on the market, how they're usually attached, as well as the distinction between an amputation above the knee (also known as "AK"), below the knee ("BK"), or a double BK (missing both legs below the knee). "When you're an AK," he said, "you have less leverage to move yourself around than you do when you're a BK." The lingo was strange, like we were ordering at a fast-food restaurant: *I'll have a double BK with fries on the side.*

Our first meeting was short—just an introduction. I thanked Kevin for coming by and we scheduled a follow-up. As he left, I thought about what Dr. Canale had already told me: If I ended up losing my legs, it would be below the knee—not above it. So just seeing that Kevin seemed so positive, so normal, even as an AK, gave me a small hope that losing my legs wouldn't have to be the end of the road.

Later that same evening, Brad, my snowboard friend, stopped by. I told him it was looking more likely that I'd lose my legs. He paused, looked down at the floor, then looked directly at me. "Well," he said, "look at it this way, Amy: At least when you go snowboarding, you'll never get cold feet again." We both chuckled. "Yeah, you're right," I said.

"And, I mean, when you think about it, it's kinda cool: You're gonna be challenged with learning to snowboard and walk again. Isn't that a little exciting? You know you can do it. You just have to find a way."

I hadn't thought of it like that before, but now that Brad had reframed it, it did sound like a cool experience, though the word *exciting* might've been a stretch. I loved his attitude. For more than a month, I'd heard nothing but doom and gloom.

The next morning, Dr. Canale came and stood at the foot of

my bed. The sad look on his face said everything. "We need to do the surgery," he said. "And we need to do it tomorrow. If we wait any longer, then I'll have to amputate farther up your leg. I'm going to ask Kevin to come in for the surgery," he said. It's a rarity for a prosthetist to be invited into an operating room, but Dr. Canale wanted to be sure he did the surgery in such a way that the athletic prosthetics would fit as well as they could.

Upon hearing this news, my parents were a mess. "Well, I guess it has to be done," said my mom, holding back tears. "I just wish there was something else we could do to save her legs." I know it may sound hard to believe, but I felt ready: Ready to get out of the hospital. Ready to never have another needle poked in my arm. Ready to just get rid of these legs so I could get new ones and finally move on with my life—however easy or hard that life might be.

The next day around noon, Kevin arrived with several different types of prosthetic legs—Dr. Canale wanted him to line them up in the surgery room. My family walked alongside me as the nurses wheeled me down the hall toward the OR. We passed the nurses' station, and all my nurses were too emotional to make eye contact with us. I was scared shitless, and the only way I could think of to *not* lose my mind was to create something to strive for after this was over. So as the gurney rolled closer to the operating room, I made three goals, an actual mental checklist:

Number one: I will never feel sorry for myself. I could've died that day in surgery. I was offered an easy way out, and I chose to come back. I am not a victim.

Number two: I will snowboard again this upcoming season. I haven't missed a single season since I began snowboarding, and

I'm not going to miss one now. I don't know how I'll do it, but I will find a way.

Number three: Once I figure this out, I will help others. I visualize myself sharing my story in some way. I don't know where or how—but I will. I want to show others that life does go on.

How I knew life would go on, I can't tell you. I just had faith that it would. So that was that—I created the list in my head, and then I set it aside so I could get through the operation. We rounded the corner into the pre-surgery area, and Kevin was waiting there. He was already in his scrubs. "How ya doing?" he asked. "I'm ready," I told him. "All right then," he said, giving me a thumb raise. "Let's do this."

Hold on a sec: Did I say I was *ready*? Well, maybe not completely. Because when I finally got wheeled into that freezing-cold OR, I spotted the table with all the tools that would be used for the surgery. A sheet covered them. I imagined the large, shiny saw with the round electric blade that would be used to slice through my skin and bones. My leg was to be cut at an angle, through the tibia and fibula. The nurses got me 100 percent flat on the operating table and then strapped down my hands, legs, and chest. "You're going to feel a burning sensation in your arm," the anesthesiologist told me as she put the medicine in my IV to put me under. I counted backward from ten. "Ten . . . nine . . . eight," and then just like that I was out. Cold.

The surgery was surprisingly short, less than two hours. Once they removed my feet and ankles, they cauterized the arteries and veins and nerve endings, then stapled up the skin. Before my parents knew it, I was in recovery. When I woke up, the lights in my room were dim. It was dark outside. I was groggy and my nose itched from all the anesthesia. The doctor had given me a spinal block, so I was numb from the waist down. I looked down toward my legs but couldn't see anything except for bandages.

As always, my parents were right there when I opened my eyes. "You made it through, sweet pea," my dad said. Mom later told me that after Dr. Canale had completed the surgery, he came out of the OR weeping. "Amy did just fine," he said as he cried and hugged them. He was just so heartbroken that he had to take my legs. Especially since I was just nineteen. And especially since we'd all fought so hard to save my legs—and, we thought, my best chance at a fulfilling life.

A FEW DAYS after the surgery, the bandages were ready to come off. The nurse came to my room, pulled off my sheets, and began slowly unwrapping the gauze. "Let's get a look at how you're healing," she said.

I felt very nervous to see my legs. Would they be messy? Would my legs hurt? And what would my legs look like? One layer at a time, the nurse unwrapped the white gauze. As she did so, it felt like she was ripping a set of big Band-Aids off an unshaven leg. *Rip. Rip. Rip. Rip.* Then, at last, there they were, what remained of both my legs. Dr. Canale came in to examine me.

Though my skin was covered in a bit of brown, dried blood, the stapled incisions looked neat and clean, like two smiley faces when I looked down over them. "They're actually looking pretty good," the doctor concluded. I agreed. I wasn't sure what to expect—but the skin seemed a lot more healed than I thought it would be.

Another pleasant surprise: I had more leg left than I'd envisioned: Below my knee, I still had my full calf muscles and about ten inches left of my shin. As promised, Dr. Canale had carefully chosen to amputate at just the right length, one that would pair up well with the prosthetic options Kevin had chosen for me. "Well, I'm satisfied with the progress," said Dr. Canale. "Let's wrap you back up for now." "Dr. Canale?" I asked before he left that day. "Yes?" he said. "Once I heal and get my new legs—how long do you think it'll be before I can go back to work?" He paused. "Well," he said, "if everything goes well, you may be able to go back in a year." *A whole year?* He might as well have told me it would be in my next lifetime. I craved going back to work.

Just about every day after that, the nurses checked in with me: "How are your stumps today?" they'd ask. I was like, *My stumps? What am I, a tree?* I'd answer with, "My *legs* are fine, thank you." I wanted to feel as normal as I possibly could—and the word *stump* somehow made me feel like an object, rather than a human being. To this day, I thoroughly dislike labels, and I rarely use the word *amputee*. It implies that I have lost something. I am not a "stump" or an "amputee." I am Amy Michelle Purdy. Period.

Finally, about a week after the surgery, all of the bandages were removed. At last, some fresh air. One evening, the first ever that I lay there, bandage-free, the lights were off. My dad had fallen asleep in the chair beside me. My mom and Crystal were down the hall resting. The light from the television flickered, offering just enough light for me to see the room around me. I tried to scoot myself up in the bed a little, but I couldn't—I no longer had any feet to help me shift. Every day for years, I'd used more than one hundred different muscles, bones, and ligaments in my feet to walk, to step, to balance, to sit down or get up, to scoot, to make so many micro-adjustments I never used to think about. "The human foot is a masterpiece of engineering and a work of art," Leonardo da Vinci once said. I no longer had a masterpiece to even help me prop myself up on my knees.

I looked down at my legs. *Is this what my life's going to be like?* I thought. *Will I really be able to do all the things I love, like travel, snowboard, massage?* My goals and passions hadn't shifted, but the ground beneath me had. I was still myself, I just no longer had the legs to carry me toward my dreams. The reality of that began hitting me, and it hurt. I thought of that boy Mom once told me about—the nineteen-year-old who suddenly lost his legs. My mother later discovered that he'd been hit with the exact same form of meningitis that I had. In a million years, I never would've predicted that that guy's story would become my own. We live as if we know how everything will turn out. I certainly lived that way. But we don't know anything. Really, we don't. To think otherwise is at best arrogant and at worst foolish.

I wasn't sad in this moment. I was fearful. Afraid of what my life was going to look like. Not wanting to get into a negative mind space, I decided to close my eyes and think about the things I loved, like snowboarding. I visualized myself carving down the mountain. The powder beneath my board. The stillness of the trees. The wind on my face. The muscles twitching in my legs. I let myself fall into a daydream so deep and so strong that I actually felt as if I were having the actual experience. I could feel the wind against my face, the beat of my racing heart, the adrenaline coursing through my entire body. In this vision, I got down to the bottom of the hill and pulled up my pant leg. I saw a prosthetic—there it was, strapped to my board. And in that moment, in my dream, I knew that if I could envision something so powerfully, then there was the possibility that it could become real. I reached for the nearby remote, turned off the television, and drifted off to sleep with that thought firmly planted in my head.

CHAPTER 8

Home

"Faith is taking the first step even when you
don't see the whole staircase."

—DR. MARTIN LUTHER KING JR.

My dad drove me home in his big truck in the second week of September. Between my hospital stay and a short stint in rehab, I'd been away for nearly two months. I couldn't wait to sleep in my own bed.

Even the last part of my hospital stay was tough. One day while watching a movie with Crystal, I lost 85 percent of my hearing in my left ear. There was sound, and then—all in an instant— near silence; hearing loss is common among meningitis survivors. Also, I had a quarter-size hole in my right cheek and multiple scars on my face where my skin died from the septic shock. I had a dialysis port implanted and a tube taped to my upper arm. Yet the way I saw it, for each loss, there was a gain: My hands had survived, so I could still paint and massage. My nose had healed, so I could smell the desert rain. I had more of my legs than I'd expected to keep. And most important, I had my life. It all could have been so much worse.

On the day my dad rolled me out of rehab I sat in a rickety wheelchair. Once we got to the truck, he picked up my broken body and gently placed me in the passenger-side seat. It's weird to have someone carry you when you're used to being able to walk. My father buckled me in. I felt so small, like a vulnerable little girl. Before I entered the hospital, I stood a strong 125 pounds and five feet six, and then, thanks to that fifty pounds of saline, I ballooned to 175 pounds. On the day I left the hospital, I weighed a mere 83 pounds, which is about how much I weighed in fifth grade. Total skin and bones—that's the state I was in when I came back to the real world.

My dad turned onto the long dirt road leading up to our house. My mind flashed back to the evening when I'd last traveled that road, gasping for oxygen as Michelle raced us to the hospital in full panic mode. Everything looked so different now—the cactuses, the sand-colored dirt, the dust and tumbleweeds. Nothing around me had truly changed. But because I felt so different, my view of things had shifted. So much had happened.

My mom and Crystal were home and awaiting my arrival. "Amelia's home!" my mom yelled as my dad wheeled me in through the front door. She leaned down and kissed me on the check. Crystal ran over and embraced me. "Hi, sissy," she said, smiling. The house smelled like my mom's amazing chicken and dumplings. "We haven't touched a thing since you left here," my mom said. "It's all exactly the same." I glanced around to notice the row of water jugs, one of which I'd grabbed on my way out. Then my dad rolled me into my bedroom, and there, next to my futon, was my row of shoes—several pairs of Vans, flip-flops, and the pair of high heels I'd just bought. *I won't be needing those.*

After dinner, Mom ran some warm water and helped me off my wheelchair and down into the bathtub. By this point, my whole family, including Dad, had seen every inch of me, so I had little inhibition left. If anything, I wanted to protect *them* from seeing how wasted away I was, because I knew how much that broke their hearts. As Mom lowered me into the tub, she had to be careful not to get the dialysis port wet. Once she situated me perfectly, all I can say is . . . *Aaaah.* I love baths. While in the hospital, I daydreamed about this moment.

As I watched the water sway around what was left of my body, all I could think about was how skinny I was. How purple the scar was from my sternum to my belly button. How my hip bones and ribs stuck out. *Is this the same body that used to be so strong and healthy?* I hardly even recognized myself. After I'd soaked for a half hour, my mom came in and scrubbed my back. She then hoisted me from the tub, dried me off, and dressed me for bed. Soon after, I got my second *aaaah:* my room, my bed, my sheets. Just to lie there in familiar surroundings felt incredible.

Day one—my first full day at home. How would I spend my time? I'd been counting down the minutes until I could go home— but now that I was there, I realized there wasn't much I could do without the help of my mother, who'd stopped working just to take care of me full-time. So I slept quite a bit. I also watched my share of television. That first day and for months to come, one of my favorites was *Oprah,* which came on daily at 4 P.M. Back in 1999, the show always ended with this segment I loved called "Remem-

bering Your Spirit"—a little story about how someone had overcome a difficulty, learned a lesson, or been inspired in some way.
Eckhart Tolle, a spiritual teacher, was also a frequent guest. "The
past has no power over the present moment," Eckhart often said.
In light of the trauma I'd just been through, that was such a powerful statement—straight from the TV set to my heart. I couldn't
get enough of *Oprah*.

One afternoon, I asked my mom to run out and pick up some
Jamba juice, one of the only things I could keep down. When she
returned, carrying the drink, I asked her a random question.

"Mom?"

"Yes, sweetie?"

"I've been thinking about something."

"Sure, Amy. What is it?"

"Um . . ." I paused. "Am I disabled now?"

My mom put down the cup and walked over to sit down on the
edge of the couch right next to me. "Listen, honey," she said. "By
some people's standards, yes: You are disabled." She stopped for a
second before finishing her thought. "But to me—you will never
be 'disabled.' You're not a label, you're my daughter. And I believe
you can do anything you put your mind to."

I didn't respond. I was still trying to make sense of my new
reality—of not only what it would mean to, say, crawl my way
from my bed to the restroom in the middle of the night, but also
how I'd be perceived. Would people see me in the same way I saw
the Vietnam vet at the side of the road? Would they pity me?
Would they view me as "the girl without legs"? Would they bother
to get to know the real me? In the hospital, I hadn't even let myself
think about those kinds of questions—my big goal was just to get

well and get home. But now that I was home with nothing but time to think, the hard questions began surfacing.

Before I could think myself into a stupor, I could usually count on Crystal to lighten the mood. A few days after that conversation with my mom, I told my sister what we'd talked about—and I admitted my fear of how I'd be perceived. "Well, people might call you 'handicapped,'" she said, "but that's crazy because you still have hands. Actually, you're really *foot*-dicapped!" We both laughed. It didn't change my situation, but it did make me smile a little and forget, even just for a minute, that I was lying there without legs.

Once home from the hospital, I began dialysis, which is a treatment used to remove harmful substances from the blood when your own kidneys can no longer do so. I was scheduled to go three mornings a week, and my mom got us up and out by 5 A.M. For me, dialysis was basically 240 minutes of sleep and complete nausea, all while being surrounded by people five times my age. No one in that place was under eighty. Seriously. Then once I was home, the physical effects lingered: On the couch, I lay quivering, vomiting, and feeling dehydrated for a couple more hours.

I usually slept from 9 A.M. to noon, and when I awakened, I tried to keep myself busy and distracted from the nausea. I did a lot of reading. One of my favorite books was *The Alchemist,* which is about finding your passion and chasing your dreams. I also read passages from the Tao Te Ching, an ancient Chinese philosophy; other times, I flipped through a *National Geographic* or checked out a nature or travel documentary on the Discovery Channel. I figured that if I couldn't get out in the world on my own, I would find other ways to experience the outdoors. Witnessing people climb mountains, sail oceans, and travel the world made me all the more eager to get up off my couch and onto my new legs, Not long after, Kevin would begin showing me how I could.

THE WEDDING WAS still on for October 15. Crystal and Jared had nearly postponed it. But since I was out of the hospital in September (and since they would've taken a major loss on the money they'd already invested), they chose to go ahead with the celebration. By the time I came home, they had a little over a month to somehow pull everything together. Crystal was still having second thoughts about moving forward with everything. Around the house, I overheard her asking my mom, "Should we be doing this? Is it right?" One time, she brought it up to me directly: "Amy, are you okay with this?" I reassured her that I was.

My sister's life became a whirlwind. As I dozed on the sofa, Miss Organized was usually down on the floor, working away on another wedding-related task, like hand-making the wedding favors—she's very craft-y. The wedding and reception were going to be at our home, out in the backyard, right at dusk; my family planned on cooking for the three hundred guests who'd been invited. While I was still in the hospital, Crystal had asked me to be her maid of honor. As you can imagine, my mom—who was clearly already busy with transitioning me home—was also moving nonstop to get our house ready.

Meanwhile, in the middle of all the wedding preparation, my big prosthetic appointment finally arrived in late September. *What will my new legs look like?* I wondered. I had no idea, really. Kevin had shown me his leg (lots of metal and screws), but because he's an AK, I knew my legs wouldn't necessarily look like his. I couldn't wait to finally see.

Entering Kevin's office was like rolling into a secret world. The waiting room looked sterile and clinical—a check-in desk and the waiting room were lit by fluorescent overhead lights. Inspirational posters of athletes who wore prosthetics—weight lifters, runners, bikers—lined the walls; none of the pictures featured an athlete who'd lost *both* legs. A bunch of industry magazines—publications filled with stories about life with prosthetics, plus listings of gatherings and events for those who'd lost their legs—were spread out on the waiting room table. Three or four older people with prosthetics were sitting around in chairs; when I came in, they all looked up and stared, which made me feel embarrassed. I wanted to yell, "I'm not an amputee! I'm a frickin' massage therapist and a snowboarder!" But I stayed quiet.

Kevin rounded the corner. "Hello, Amy!" He was as upbeat as he was the day I met him in the hospital. "Come on in—I'm glad you're here."

Mom wheeled me into this big room where some industrial tools had been laid out on a shelf—scissors, a hammer, a huge metal shoehorn.

"We're going to cast your legs today," he said. As I sat in my wheelchair and my mom looked on, he wrapped both my legs in the same kind of casting material you'd be wrapped in if you broke a limb; in order to fit me with prosthetics, he first had to take this mold, he said. "The idea is to end up with a socket that's the shape of your leg," he explained as he worked. After a half hour, he stood up.

"Okay, Amy. You're all done for today. I'll see you next week."

I left hoping that our second appointment would be as easy as the first.

It wasn't. One afternoon the following week, I again arrived at Kevin's office, this time to see my new legs. I was excited. How many times in life can you say, "I'm going down to pick up my legs today"? It sounded so strange and funny. "Hey, Mom, let's go get my legs!" I'd joked all week. Mom and I both cracked up.

On my second visit, Kevin met us in a different room, an open space with two parallel walking bars. My mom wheeled me over near the bar. When Kevin walked in, he was carrying these two big, clear, bulky hunks of plastic with metal pipes attached. "Your legs are ready!" he announced. My heart nearly fell out of my chest. *Those couldn't be my legs.* He sat them down.

I hadn't been quite sure what to expect, but I certainly wasn't expecting what I saw. My new "legs" looked more like hollow buckets. The "ankle" was a set of pipes bolted together. The "foot" was yellow and rubber. The "toes" were square and masculine. From the toe down to the ankle, there was a raised yellow line that was supposed to resemble a vein. The legs couldn't have looked more fake. There was nothing mechanical, high-tech, bionic, or cool about them. They looked like they'd come directly out of a hardware store. They were hideous.

"Um . . . are these my starter legs?" I asked, widening my eyes to the size of two silver dollars. Inside, I was screaming, "You've got to be kidding me!" I was horrified at the thought that these two hollow hunks of hardware could be my new legs . . . *forever.* Tears streamed down my cheeks. That set off my mom, who started bawling, too.

"It's okay, it's okay," Kevin said in as soothing a voice as he could muster. "This is just the beginning. This is going to be a process. Let's just give it a shot and see if we can get you up and moving on these."

Before he put on my legs, Kevin pulled out a pair of green and gray liners; they looked like socks, only heavier, about a quarter of an inch thick and very nonbreathable. On the inside, the liners were sticky in order to make them adhere to my leg. "These are like cushiony shock absorbers that will protect your shins and knees from friction while they're in your new legs," Kevin explained. He unrolled one of the heavy polyurethane liners, slid its base onto the bottom of my leg, then unrolled it all the way up to the middle of my thigh; he did the same with the second one. On top of that, he put on another layer, a second thick wool sock; then after he slid on my prosthetic leg, he added a third layer, a sleeve that both kept my leg on and suffocated it at the same time. It must have been 85 degrees that day—and suddenly it felt like 105.

"Okay," coached Kevin. "I'll help you stand up in these." With both my new feet on the floor, I stood up. *Crap.* As my full body bore down on the legs, my knees, my calves, and the bottom of my legs began throbbing. Not only were my legs in killer pain, but they also felt very confined and restricted under all those layers of socks and sleeves. I couldn't even bend my knees. All my blood rushed down to the bottom of my legs. Every nerve in my legs was screaming, "Stop!" The discomfort and pressure were nearly unbearable. More tears flowed. After standing for only a few seconds, I flopped back down in the wheelchair.

Kevin gave me a minute to regroup. "Okay, now let's try it again," he finally said. He helped me up and practically carried me to the nearby bar. I placed my hand on the rail and tried to steady myself. "See if you can take a step," he said. I leaned forward. "Oh my God, it hurts so bad!" I shouted. I must've stood there for a full five minutes before, at last—*clunk*—I managed to take one tiny step. "That's great, Amy," he said. "Now try to take another step." I struggled to lift my right leg, but it felt like my thighs had been cemented down into a massive block. I strained again to lift it, and then—*clunk*—another step.

"I think that's enough for today," Kevin said, realizing that was the most he was going to get out of me. "Remember, this is part of the process. You have to start getting comfortable with these legs. I know it's very hard for you to walk in them, but we'll get through this a little at a time. You may have to go through five sets of legs this year before you get a pair that even fit right." He explained that, as your body changes and your legs atrophy, you often have to be refitted. Kevin was doing his best—which is what any great prosthetist would have done. Yet the prosthetics were so ugly that I wouldn't have even wanted to be buried in them.

My mom and I waited in the lobby as Kevin packed up the legs and prepared what he called a care package: a bag filled with those horrible liners. He also sent me home with a walker, the type you see elderly people leaning on. The plan was for me to practice walking at home, then come back to see him periodically to make adjustments to the prosthetics; he also connected me with some physical therapists in the area so they could help me adjust to walking in the new legs. "You can't just avoid putting them on," Kevin told me just before I left, "or you'll never get used to wearing them." I didn't respond. Mom wheeled me out the door while I balanced these two chunky, rubber, yellowish legs in my lap. I was not one with these legs. Not even close.

Did I mention I'd previously never let myself fall into depression? Well, in this one afternoon, that all went out the window. Emotionally, I shut down. I crawled into bed feeling so overwhelmed that I couldn't even think straight. This. Was. My. Life. And I hated it. Not only were these new legs ugly as hell; they were also about as indelicate as anything I'd ever laid eyes on. Kevin had simply chosen the legs he thought would get me up on my feet, and that wasn't about fashion or femininity. It was 100 percent about function. But how was I supposed to fit these beastly things into my new life? Especially on summer weekends, I lived in my flip-flops and shorts. And forget about snowboarding, I wasn't even sure I could learn to *walk* in these legs.

My mom and I drove home in silence. Not a single word. When she got me into the house and wheeled me in, we each went into our rooms and curled up with the dried tears still covering our faces. *How the hell am I going to do this?* was my final thought before I escaped into sleep. That evening, I slept for eleven hours straight. Seriously.

A heavy cloud hung over me the next morning. And the next. And the next.

I slid into a terrible mood. If I had to name the biggest freak-out episode I had during this entire experience, this would be it. As usual, my mom and I had to keep getting up at 4 A.M. for dialysis, and I remained quiet through all of it. Post-dialysis, I sank into the couch and passed out for another round of sleep. I didn't even want to be awake long enough to think about my predicament.

Around five o'clock one evening a few days after I'd gotten my new legs, I woke up just as overwhelmed as I'd been when I'd fallen asleep. The legs were propped up on the couch; the liners sat there next to them. I glanced over at them, then away again. After a few moments, I slid over to the edge of the couch and pulled out the liners. I picked them up and looked them over for a couple of minutes. I then slid them on, one at a time, over my knees and thighs. I stumbled up to my feet and held on to a wall to steady myself. I stood there. They were still painful. I took them off and went back to sleep.

The next morning, I reached for the liners again. "I laid those out for you last night," said Mom, who came in to check on me right then. "Thanks," I mumbled. I pulled on the sticky liner. It was ice cold. I wrinkled my face. "Maybe I can heat them up a little," my mom said. I gave them to her, and she headed off to the kitchen to put them in the oven for a few seconds. She returned and handed them back to me.

I put on the rest of my liners, and my mom helped me out of the bed and up on my legs. I held on to her arm for a second to get my balance. "Can you try it again, Amy—can you take a step?" I slowly lifted my right leg. *One.* A few seconds later, I lifted my left. *Two.* Then I picked up my right leg again. *Three.* By the fourth step, I'd nearly reached my bedroom door. "That's progress," said my mom, who always tried to sound encouraging. I was still wobbly and extremely uncomfortable, but four steps was definitely better than none. Maybe I could do this.

Here's the thing about me: Even when I'm depressed, I can only stay in that mental space for so long, or else I drive myself crazy. I get sick and tired of being sick and tired. My legs and feet were never coming back, and that was just something I had to slowly begin to accept. So as much as I disliked the prosthetics, as unattractive and painful as I thought they were, I knew Kevin was right: I needed to at least *try* to get used to wearing them. What was my alternative? Yes, I could've just taken the easy way out and never made the effort, but then what kind of life would I have? I'd never been a quitter. And I didn't want to become one.

That evening in bed, I lay there and thought about my circumstances. Everything I'd been through that summer. How simple and carefree my life had been before I ended up in the hospital. How low I'd been over the previous few days. How emotionally drained I'd become. How completely out of control I felt. That's when a critical question entered my head: *If my life were a book, and I were the author, how would I want my story to go?* I lay there for another few minutes, envisioning the list of goals I'd always had for myself. I wanted to snowboard. I wanted to travel. I wanted to learn, discover, and grow. I wanted stories to tell. I wanted to live a life with absolutely no regrets. The truth is, I wanted exactly the same life I'd dreamed about before this whole ordeal began, and if I wanted that life, I knew I'd have to write a new story that included new legs. I had a blank slate and a choice to make. And that night, in the shadowy light of my bedroom, I decided I would move forward as courageously as I could.

Another thing that has always been true about me: When I decide to do something, I usually throw myself into it, the same way I did when I moved to Salt Lake City. Total immersion. So I got up and put on the legs every single morning. Then day by day, I forced myself to stay in the legs a little bit longer. I gave myself mini goals, like getting down part of our hallway. Or walking from my bed to the bathroom. Or making my way from the couch to the counter. Or walking outside along the back porch, after squeezing those square toes into my Vans. I knew that in order for my mind and body to accept these legs, I had to *make* myself get used to them. I also needed a goal, so I gave myself a huge one. I wasn't going to wheel down the aisle as my sister's maid of honor. I was going to *walk*.

"I need your help," I told my physical therapist on the first day we met. "My sister's wedding is next week, and I need to be walking by then." Even to me, that sounded ambitious, since Crystal's wedding was so close. But the last thing I wanted was to have all our friends and family pitying me on my sister's big day; they'd already been feeling sorry for me for two and a half months straight, and I was over the attention. All the guests who'd be coming to the wedding had certainly heard the headline: "Amy Purdy lost her legs and almost died." That didn't need to be the focus anymore. I didn't tell Crystal or my dad about my goal to walk to the altar. I just quietly made the vow in my heart. Over the next several days, I worked my ass off.

Once I began wearing my legs more often, clothing became an issue. Since the legs were so bulky, especially in the knee area with all those thick liners, I had to buy oversized khaki pants that were big enough to fit over my knees. Or I'd have to buy pants that were two sizes too big to drape over my size-zero body. I found that one of the most uncomfortable things about having prosthetics is having to dress around them. Can you imagine being stuck in a muumuu for the rest of your life? That's what having prosthetics felt like at the beginning: You have a permanent accessory, and everything you wear must work with it or around it.

Prosthetic legs may not have been the most attractive items in my closet, but that doesn't mean they're cheap. The average cost of a set of legs is thirty thousand dollars. I'm so grateful that I had help with the cost. Just before I got sick, my mom had dropped me from her insurance plan because I was transferring to my work's plan. When I checked into the ER, I wasn't yet covered by my new plan, but because I entered the hospital in full kidney failure, Medicare and Medicaid kicked in to cover the enormous expense. So in one sense, the kidney failure was a blessing: Because of my kidney failure, most of my costs were covered. I've always tried to look at the bright side.

On the night before the wedding, my family sat around the living room, relaxing to some of our favorite music on the radio. I was in my wheelchair with my legs on, and those enormous khaki pants over them. An old country song my parents loved came on, and my father walked over to the couch and pulled my mom to her feet. "Wanna dance, sweetheart?" My mother, laughing a little, said, "Sure." The two had always danced so beautifully together; their favorite was the two-step, which is the dance they did that evening; my father led so well. My sister and I clapped for them as the song finished. Next, an Alan Jackson song came on—"Chasin' That Neon Rainbow."

I wanted to show my sister and my father how much progress I'd made. "Dad, can I dance with you?" My father smiled and looked a little shocked. "Sure, sweet pea," he said, exchanging a quick look with my mom, as if to say, "Is this for real?" I stood up slowly from the wheelchair and he pulled me toward him. We clasped hands. With the song filling our living room, my father and I swayed back and forth—and I began to two-step, moving my feet along to the music. My mom grabbed the video camera. "Amy's dancing before she's even *walking*!" Mom yelled out. As Dad and

I moved to the song's rhythm, I caught a look at my sister's face. "Oh my God, Amy—look at that! You're dancing!" My eyes filled with water as the song came to an end. "Yeah . . . I did a good job," I whispered. I hadn't just taken a couple steps. I'd danced an entire dance. Unbelievable.

Wedding day arrived. Crystal used my parents' room, which had double doors that opened up right onto the back porch, as a dressing area for the entire bridal party. My mom helped me get into my dress, being careful not to hit my dialysis port as she zipped up the dress around my skinny body. Crystal chose a long dress for me so my legs would be covered. The dress was beautiful: a pale green satin gown. It was the kind of dress you'd normally wear with dainty heels, but I couldn't, of course, because of my new flat, clunky hunks of rubber for feet. I wore white skateboard shoes. As you can imagine, they didn't look great—but at least I could walk in them. And since my life had turned into function over fashion, I was grateful.

As the guests took their seats outside, the violinists began playing "Time to Say Goodbye," the sweet Andrea Bocelli tune, which reminded me of how much I missed my job. The song was known as the Bellagio song, and every time I walked through the halls of the Bellagio to do another massage, it reverberated through the halls and elevators. It was crazy to think how much my life had changed in such a short amount of time.

Still seated in my wheelchair, I picked up my bouquet and motioned for my sister to come close to me.

"What is it?" she said, leaning down so she could hear me. Crystal always looked gorgeous—but on this day, she was stunning in her strapless white gown, which was covered in little white daisies.

"I'm not going out there in this wheelchair," I told her. "I'm walking."

She looked me directly in the eyes. "Are you sure, Amy?" she asked.

I didn't hesitate. "Yes," I said. "I will walk." Our friend Johnny, the best man, had been standing there, waiting to wheel me out. When we told him about the change of plans, he went off to find my cousin Jack, and returned with him. The two helped me up to my feet.

The sun began setting. As the violinists played in the soft light of the warm desert, the double doors to my parents' bedroom finally opened. With Johnny on one arm and Jack on the other, I moved toward the doorway. "You ready?" said Johnny. "I'm ready." A hush fell over the crowd.

I took my first step. I then stopped and looked out over all the faces. All eyes were fixed on the three of us. After a few seconds, I tightened my fingers around the bouquet and then took another step. And a third. And a fourth. One mechanical step at a time, I walked all the way from our porch, down through a little grassy area, down eight steps, and then, at last, through the aisle. My steps were slow and not as graceful as I'd hoped, and a couple of times, I had to pause because I was sore. But I kept going. And by the time I got to the altar, there was not a dry eye in our backyard.

As Crystal took her spot at the doorway, people had already pulled out their Kleenex. From my spot at the altar, I watched my sister make her grand entrance. Once she reached the altar, she and Jared exchanged their vows. And for twenty minutes (yes, twenty), I stood there, on my own two feet, and cried tears of joy for both of them.

Once the ceremony was finished, there was only one thing left to do—party. My dad had installed a dance floor in the backyard, and the DJ played all the best dance hits as our friends enjoyed plates of prime rib. "Wanna dance?" my friend Rob asked. He'd agreed to be my "date" for the wedding. "Absolutely," I said. He helped me to my feet and led me over to the dance floor. I might not have been able to do any major dance moves, but I could definitely move my body from side to side, just like I'd done with my dad the night before.

So I danced as much as I could—for a half a song—and then sat back in my wheelchair until I felt strong enough to take the floor again. All evening, friends and family came over to my table to talk with me. "I just can't believe it!" one lady said. "How is it even possible that you're walking already?" All I could do was smile and remember how unlikely this day had seemed after that first appointment with Kevin. What a difference two weeks and some serious determination makes.

My entrance at the wedding that day, my small miracle in the desert, had at one point seemed unfathomable. The bold dreams I still envisioned for myself—returning to work, getting back on a snowboard, and moving ahead with the life I'd always planned— were the bigger miracles yet unseen. But on October 15, 1999, those wild dreams suddenly felt just a little more possible. With one baby step down an aisle, I'd written the opening lines of my new story. Maybe other glorious chapters could indeed follow.

CHAPTER 9

New Season

"The secret to a rich life is to have more beginnings than endings."
—DAVID WEINBAUM

H ello?"

"Yes, miss," said the woman on the phone. I pressed my good ear close to the receiver so I could catch her every word. "How may I help you?"

"This is Amy Purdy," I said. "I have two prosthetic legs, and I want to snowboard. Has anyone in your organization ever worked with or even met a snowboarder who has two prosthetic legs?"

Long pause. "Um, I don't believe we have," said the woman. "There are skiers, of course, and if you're a double leg amputee, you could try a sit-ski."

"Thanks, but I don't ski," I said. "And I don't want to sit. I want to use my legs."

"Well, sorry, ma'am," she said, "but I can't help you."

Between the close of 1999 and the spring of 2000, I'd set out on a major search: I wanted to find at least one person in the country who'd snowboarded on two prosthetic legs. So I went online and found the phone numbers of every adaptive ski school or organization I could find—and I called all of them. And all of them seemed to have the exact same answer: "We've never met a snowboarder with a prosthetic leg before."

The ski season was coming to a close—and I wanted to keep my promise to myself to snowboard before the end of it. My plan had been to talk with someone—anyone—who'd experienced snowboarding on a prosthetic leg. I had so many questions about what legs I could use, how it might feel, and what adjustments would have to be made. But since I couldn't find such a person, I realized that I'd just have to get out on the slopes and try it for myself—whether or not I felt ready.

Since the wedding, I'd become stronger by the month. In December 1999, I switched from hemodialysis to peritoneal dialysis. Doctors removed the dialysis port, and then during another surgery, they implanted a soft plastic catheter tube into my stomach. The change made all the difference: Peritoneal dialysis is a much more gentle process that doesn't strip you of your minerals and nutrients. That meant I wasn't nearly as tired. I didn't feel nauseous. And every morning, I had enough energy to get up and put on my legs. My weight was still hovering around eighty-five pounds, but the vomiting had stopped. And best of all, peritoneal dialysis could be done at home, overnight, by hooking my stomach tube to a machine about the size of a typewriter. The switch was a major turning point for me. I could actually function.

I'd also been doing everything I could to make my legs more

comfortable. I spent countless hours in Kevin's office, having him adjust the prosthetics. The entire process felt like two steps forward, one step back: He'd grind out an area to relieve some pressure to my leg, and I'd leave his office feeling good. But then a couple of days later, I'd be walking around the grocery store and I'd start feeling very sore again—remember, this is a hard-as-steel carbon fiber socket rubbing against your bone and soft tissue. There's nothing high-tech about it; it's actually barbaric. So I'd get home later to find a raw wound, and I'd then have to stay off my legs until Kevin could make another adjustment. It was very frustrating. But by spring 2000, after too many adjustments to mention, I was finally able to stay in my legs for most of a day—and I wanted to try snowboarding again at least once.

"Why don't we just go over to Lee Canyon and try a run?" Brad said to me one afternoon in March 2000. He and the other guys had been snowboarding all season—and Brad knew how eager I'd been to get out onto the slopes again. "That sounds great," I said. "Let's head over there this weekend." I knew if I didn't just go for it, I probably never would. So my sister and I drove up and met him one Saturday morning. I wore my basic walking legs and packed all of my usual gear. The whole way there, I kept thinking, *What is this going to feel like?*

We hiked our way up a hill to the chairlift. Walking in bulky snow boots felt awkward—Kevin had set up my feet to walk in my Vans, and I was suddenly in a boot with a different design, heel, and sole. I quickly discovered that these legs weren't going to adapt to different conditions, so I would have to.

At the top of the hill, I strapped my left foot onto the board and kept my back foot free so I could push off it. We got up onto the chairlift. As my leg dangled with the weight of the board on it, I realized my leg was slipping. *Crap—my whole leg could fall off right now.* The only thing keeping my leg on was the sleeve, and I could feel it coming loose. So I kicked both my legs up on the seat and sat sideways so my legs and board could rest on the seat. "You okay?" Crystal was holding on to me as I held onto the bar. "Yeah, I'm good," I said. I didn't want to make a scene.

Up to that point, I'd only had one thought: *What will it be like when I snowboard?* But as the chair ascended higher up the mountain, that thought was replaced by a new one: *What if I can't snowboard?* I'd put so much energy into convincing myself that it was possible—but what if it wasn't? What if it was just too hard? That scared me, because being a snowboarder was such a huge part of who I was. I had to make this work.

We reached the top and lifted our bar. I rode down the slight, twenty-foot hill to get to the area where you fully strap on your board. On my way down, I didn't fall once. *Good start.* Normally, I'd remain standing to strap into my board—but I discovered I needed to sit because of my nonbending ankles. Brad helped me stand back up on my feet.

I began sliding down the mountain. After only about five feet, I noticed something major right off the bat: I couldn't feel the snow under my feet. I felt like I was hovering. My actual body was a foot off the ground. I adjusted my body and tried to find my balance so that I could carve on the heel edge. That worked. But here's what wasn't working: My tibias were in massive pain as the bone pushed up against the socket. And without ankle flexion, I felt like a stick man—no flexibility to get onto my toe edge, as if my entire lower body were stuck in a restrictive cast.

I picked up speed. I threw my body weight over my toe edge, and the momentum began pulling me down the mountain. *Okay, I thought, maybe I can do this.* Then about a quarter of the way down the slope, I hit a bump. Because I had zero shock absorption in my feet, my entire body catapulted into the air. My goggles went one way, my beanie went another way, and my legs—still attached to the snowboard—went flying thirty feet down the mountainside. "Oh my God!" I yelled as my sister came racing over. I was seeing stars.

When you fall off your board and your gear goes everywhere, snowboarders jokingly call that a "yard sale"—and this was the ultimate one. "Are you okay?" Crystal asked. "I think so," I said. We both laughed. By this time, Brad was already gathering my heavy legs (which were about seven pounds each, not including the weight of the board) and carrying them back up the mountain for me. People in the chairlifts above us stared down. One lady actually screamed: "Aaaah!" We were all in shock. I got back up on my feet long enough for us to get down the rest of the mountain, falling left and right along the way, but never again losing my legs. Once I made it to the bottom, we called it a day. I'd had enough.

Truthfully, my first attempt to snowboard with prosthetics was incredibly discouraging—at least initially. Yet even as I rode home, I began trying to figure some things out in my head. *How can I make this work? I have incredible pain in my tibias. My ankles don't move. My legs might come off. How could I fix that?* First of all, I'd need to find legs that fit more comfortably. I'd also need to get some ankles that moved. And of course, I'd have to find a way to keep my detachable body parts attached.

Instead of sending me into another depression, the experience forced me to find a way to resolve the issues. This is when I learned that the obstacles in our lives can only do one of two things: stop us dead in our tracks, or force us to get creative. Just months before, learning to walk in prosthetics had gone from seeming impossible to becoming possible—so maybe the same could be true for learning to snowboard in prosthetics. Maybe.

MY MOM AND I went out to a prosthetic appointment one afternoon. On our way home, we passed a strip mall with a puppy store—one where customers could go in and actually play with the puppies. "Mom, can we stop in there for a second?" I asked. "Sure." I'd been to the store with a friend months before, and I wanted to show my mom this Chihuahua I'd spotted. "You have to see him," I told her. "He's so cute." We pulled up to the store and went inside.

The Chihuahua wasn't there—but I did spot a kiddie pool full of puppy beagles. "Awww, look how adorable they are, Mom," I said, bending down to pet one. Then out of the corner of my eye, I noticed this one beagle that was yelping and frantically trying to get out. She had her paws up on the ledge of the pool. When I got up and walked around to the other side of the pool, she followed me. "Oh, she wants you to pick her up," my mom said, smiling. So I reached down and scooped her little three-pound body into my arms, and she just melted.

Well, so did I: She had the prettiest floppy, soft, caramel-colored ears. She was mostly brown and black, with little touches of white on her face, paws, and chest. She was really petite—the runt of the litter. When she looked up at me with those sweet eyes, it was like she was saying, "Take me!" My mom agreed: "It looks like she wants to go home with you," she said. I pulled the puppy up close to me, then walked over to a long mirror in the store. Her cute head and ears sank right into my shoulder, like she'd just let out a deep breath and relaxed. I loved her instantly—but I knew my dad would have a fit if I brought her home. So I reluctantly put her back down into the pool and left the store. My dad loves animals—he just doesn't love them in the house.

Early one morning a few days after I saw the puppy, I mentioned it to Crystal when she stopped by to visit me. "She was so cute!" I told her. "Then let's go back and get her," my sister said. "What?" I said. "You just lost your legs—you frickin' deserve a dog." "You know Dad's not going to go for that," I said. "You just went through hell, Amy. You deserve a dog if you want one." I hesitated—but Crystal was so convincing. Three hundred dollars later, I came home with my new love. I named her Roxy Ann Purdy.

When my dad came home later, we surprised him by leaving Roxy in the center of the living room in a box. "I just don't know about this," Dad said, trying to resist when she snuggled right up to his chest. "Well, I guess we could keep her," he finally said, giving in. "Yes!" Crystal and I shouted, high-fiving each other. "Thanks, Dad!" "Just remember," my dad said, looking directly at me, "she's your dog—so you'll have to take care of her. You'll have to feed her and let her in and out every day." I excitedly agreed.

Roxy became my angel dog—my love covered in fur. She was also my physical therapy: Every day, I arose early, pulled on those ice-cold liners, stepped into my legs, and took her outside. She was an extremely adventurous puppy: Once I opened the back door, she'd scamper all the way off into the desert, sniffing and exploring and sometimes chasing after a rabbit. She seldom stayed close to my side. Every half hour, she'd be whimpering for me to take her back outside—which meant I was forced to either stay in my legs, or put them on multiple times every day. At least twice a day, I'd have to go out into the desert and bring her back to the house. As challenging as it was to chase after her day after day, Roxy gave me a reason to keep moving—a purpose powerful enough to keep me off the couch and up on my legs.

One evening, I took Roxy outside while I was on the phone. I sat on the back porch and talked while keeping an eye on her. Just as she set her paw on the grass, a wild coyote walked up to within twenty feet of us. I paused. "Let me call you back," I said to whomever I was chatting with. I tried to grab Roxy, but she was just out of my reach. The coyote was trying to lure her in by letting her get close to him. That's what coyotes do: When there's a pack of them, they often send out one coyote to bring back a dog or other animal they can attack. When I moved toward the coyote, he bolted—and Roxy took off after him, full speed.

"Roxy, come back!" I yelled, running after her. I'd Velcro'd flip-flops onto my feet, and both of the flip-flops flew off as I hauled ass through the desert, jumping over rocks and cactuses along the way. "Nooooo!" I shouted. The coyote had grabbed Roxy by her neck and the two were rolling around in the dirt about fifty yards ahead of me. When I caught up, I began kicking the coyote as hard as I could. "Get off!" I yelled. "Go away!" After a few seconds, he dropped Roxy from his teeth and scampered off. I picked up my sweet Roxy and walked the nearly half mile back to our house—the whole way, feeling relieved that she was still alive.

"You okay, honey?" I said, pulling Roxy right up to my shoulder. She wasn't gushing blood, but she did have multiple puncture wounds on her neck. My mom had witnessed the whole scene from the back porch—she'd come out when she heard me screaming.

"Let's have the neighbor check her out," my mom said. Our neighbor was a vet, and she later came over and determined that Roxy didn't need stitches. Yet the real story of the episode wasn't how fast Roxy had run—it was how quickly I had raced across the desert in my legs. As my mom later recounted the story to my sister and dad, she said, "Here Amy is, being so careful as she walks around the house in her legs—and then she just took off *sprinting*!" I hadn't even felt my legs while I was running. I was so focused on rescuing Roxy that any pain or soreness wasn't noticeable. It proved a powerful point to me: When we're focused and determined enough, we are capable of so much.

AT THE START of summer 2000, I switched to a different kind of leg. I went from using those beginner legs with the big sleeve over my knee to prosthetics with a pin system. Long before then, I'd been wanting the pin system—but your legs first have to be fully healed before you can graduate to it. With the new leg, you first roll on a thick liner that has a two-inch pin attached at its base, then you step into the leg and the pin on the liner goes into the lock at the distal end of the socket. And—*click*—you're locked in. To take them off, you press a button toward the base and your leg releases.

This new system was a life changer for me: My legs, and especially my knees, were far more streamlined, which meant I could wear the clothes I liked. And compared to the beginner legs, they felt great—a lot more comfortable. As soon as I got the system, I began feeling more independent. I didn't have to take my legs on and off as much because I could tolerate them for the full day. I could exercise more. And I could go out and socialize with friends without drawing the stares you get when you're wearing large drawstring pants. I wanted to burn those things.

I began to realize that there were some benefits to having bionic body parts. I could adjust both my shoe size (from an 8 to a 6½ . . . the size that always seems to be on sale!) and my height. I'd been about five feet six; I could go up or down about an inch in either direction. I generally liked being taller, but depending on who I was with, where I was going, or what I was wearing, I'd customize my height and I still do to this day.

I actually made it my goal to not let my legs be a burden. I decided that my legs weren't going to be something I *had* to put on every day. They were going to be part of me. Rather than resenting the legs or seeing them as a daily chore I had to tolerate, I learned to actually embrace them—one cute pair of shoes at a time.

CHAPTER 10

The Gift

"Until we can receive with an open heart,
we are never really giving with an open heart."

—BENÉ BROWN

An old flame was coming through town. In the summer of 2000, just a few weeks after I transferred to the pin system, this guy friend of mine—a very attractive one, I might add—called me up. "I'll be visiting Vegas soon, and it would be great if we could catch up," he said. We'd never had a serious romance, just a very strong friendship, but we had made out a couple of times.

We'd first met in Salt Lake when I was massaging the men's U.S. Olympic ski team. He was on the team. And though we had not seen each other in a while because of his travel schedule, he did call my parents to check up on me when he heard I was in the hospital. When he told me he was dropping by Vegas, I was excited to see him again. Once we agreed to hang out, I think it was just mutually understood that we'd spend the night together, and the truth is that I was nervous about that. What would he think of my new body? I was still extremely thin, not to mention that I had scars I wasn't yet comfortable with. And though I did love the pin system, I was still getting used to my new legs. The thought of taking them off in front of someone else was a little scary.

When it came to my legs, I'd received a compliment not long before, some kind words that I've never forgotten. I went out to a bar with some of my guy friends, and as I was sitting there, the bottom edge of my jeans, which were creased up, revealed my shiny titanium ankle. Later, my friend Josh came over to me and said, "You know, there's something really hot about the fact that you have metal legs." "Really?" I said, smiling. "Yes," he said. "Guys love stuff like metal and duct tape and hardware and cars, so seeing your ankle slashed with metal—it's pretty damn hot." I laughed.

Even with that extra boost of confidence, I was still a little anxious on the evening when my guy friend came to town. He hadn't seen me since I'd lost so much weight. I put on jeans and a cute top. I wanted to look as close as I could to the way I looked when we were last together. I did my hair and makeup and got all dolled up and met him and a few of his friends at a bar on the Strip. "Hey, Amy!" he said, embracing me right away. "Hi!" I said. Nothing about our initial meeting felt awkward. *Relief.* I walked around the entire casino that night and didn't once think about my legs. Amazing what happens when your mind is on other things. Over drinks, we laughed and caught up, and it all flowed smoothly. We actually had a lot of fun with each other. After his friends left for the evening, he asked, "So, are you staying the night with me or what?" I smiled. We both already knew the answer. "Of course," I said. We left together.

Back in his room, we talked a bit more, and we were both ready to call it a night. I sat down on the edge of the bed while he went to brush his teeth in the bathroom. When he came out, he started taking off his shirt to get ready for bed. "Okay," I said nervously, trying to prepare him for what he was about to see. "So you know I need to take off my legs," I said. "And I have all these scars and stuff." "That's fine," he said casually. "Do whatever you have to do." He could not have seemed more cool about the whole thing.

Taking off your clothes is one thing. Taking off your clothes and your *legs* is an entirely different matter. I pulled down my jeans, unhooked myself from my legs, and left everything at the side of the bed. I was basically sitting there in my top and my underwear; I felt so vulnerable and exposed, more naked than you could ever feel. He could tell I was feeling shy. "It's okay, Amy," he said, pulling me toward him on the bed. "I don't mind." We curled up together. Without my legs on, I felt so little next to his tall, muscular body. He was extremely supportive—and of course, there was also plenty of chemistry between us.

The connection we shared that evening was amazing—and after the year I'd survived, it was also much needed. He made me feel so comfortable. At times I did feel self-conscious, but that would only last for a few seconds, and then I'd get back in the moment. Neither one of us was looking for a relationship. And though we didn't really stay in close touch in the coming years, I've always believed that we crossed each other's paths at exactly the right juncture. I needed my first experience of intimacy in this new body to be a positive one. And it was.

During the next few years, I dated a handful of other guys, and I began to realize that if I didn't focus on my "flaws," they really didn't, either. It's pretty amazing how that works. We always have a choice whether to focus on the negative or positive. That's not to say I don't have insecurities; we all do. But over time, I started to see that the things that make us unique are actually the things that make us beautiful.

A COUPLE OF weeks after that experience, I left town. After getting that portable dialysis machine, I'd become even more eager to reclaim some of the independence I'd had before I got sick. So I made plans to work at Challenge Aspen, an outdoor adventure, theater, and arts camp for differently abled children. My aunt Cindy had been dating a guy named John in Aspen and knew of the camp. "You should go up there," she said. "They would love you. You can even stay in John's condo—he'll be away for the summer." When I looked into the camp, I discovered they needed a volunteer art director for a few weeks. It sounded perfect for me. "Mom, will you take me?" I asked. She agreed, and then drove me all the way to Aspen and dropped me off at the condo. At last, full freedom.

From the moment I arrived, I was happy. I could hike as much as I wanted. The mountain air smelled so fresh. I was in charge of painting all the backdrops for the kids' theater sets, including the one for *The Wizard of Oz,* yet in the evenings, I was also free to get dressed up, walk down to the little town, meet people, and have dinner. And oh my goodness, the kids in this camp—they were the sweetest. They ranged in age from five all the way up to twelve. Some wore prosthetics and had various types of physical challenges; others had cognitive delays. A nine-year-old blond girl named Amy—I called her my "mini me," because in addition to sharing my name, she also wore two prosthetics—asked me a question one afternoon. "Amy," she said, "what do you do when people at school call you a robot?" I stopped painting for a moment and looked at her. "Well," I said, "aren't robots pretty dang cool? You're not just a robot. You're a fembot, and that's even cooler. So when they call you a robot, just say, 'Thank you.'" She smiled, and I suddenly realized that as difficult as my journey had been up to that point, I'd never had to manage it as a child. The entire experience of being at that camp was humbling and eye-opening—I have so much to be grateful for, and being around the children was a daily reminder. I realized that helping the kids was helping me.

When I returned from Aspen, I felt rejuvenated and physically stronger than ever, thanks to all that hiking and moving around. I even put on a little weight: I'd gotten up to nearly one hundred pounds. Thankfully, Canyon Ranch had agreed to let me return to my job whenever I could, and in July, I knew I was ready. Dr. Canale had been right: It took about a year of healing before I was in good enough shape to go back to work. I couldn't wait to rejoin the staff. I really missed my job.

By the time I went back to work, I'd already relearned how to drive. Right after I got my new legs, Kevin had been sure I'd need hand controls, which is a system that some people with physical challenges use if they can't maneuver the brake and gas pedals with their feet. I refused. "I won't be using hand controls," I told Kevin. "I want to use my feet." *Could it really be that hard to drive with prosthetics?*

My dad and I went out one afternoon to practice in my truck. I got in, turned the key in the ignition, and slowly pressed down on the gas pedal. *So far, so good.* A minute later, I braked. Though

I couldn't feel my feet on the bottom of the brake, I could feel the pressure of pushing against the brake with my legs. It took a few minutes of stopping and going to learn how quickly the brake or gas pedals responded when I pressed down. I drove down a dirt road, around our neighborhood, and then back home again. That was enough practice for me to pick it up. I might've been a little more cautious than usual the first couple of weeks I was on the road, but I quickly became comfortable. I certainly drove well enough to drive myself to and from work every day. From that point on, I decided I had to make my own rules. Kevin had been trying to help me, but if I had listened to him, I might never have discovered that I could drive normally.

Right away, things at work were different for me. For one thing, my feet often made a squeaking noise when I led a client from the waiting area down the long, quiet hallways. I'm sure at least a few of them noticed and thought, *Is that the floor squeaking? Or is this woman squeaking?* There I was, trying to create this peaceful Zen experience, and—*squeak*—one of my screws would make itself heard. It drove me crazy and made the hair on my arms stand up on end—but what could I do? That's the kind of experience that just comes with having mechanical body parts. I also had to stand on my feet a lot, and not just stand, but actually massage someone. That put more pressure on my legs. I dealt with it by taking a few minutes to sit and regroup between each session.

When you have prosthetics, you can never again just dash out of the house with a purse, some lipstick, and your phone. My bag was filled with all kinds of tools, because I could never be sure when a screw or bolt would come loose. Believe me, it has happened: in airports, in restaurants, on street corners. All of a sudden, I could go from walking . . . to hobbling . . . to sitting, if some of the bolts *really* became loose. Thankfully, none of that happened while I was giving a massage, but I knew it could, which is why I always left home with at least an Allen wrench.

Once I went back to work, I slowly worked my way up from three massages a day to six or seven back-to-back, plus that mile-and-a-half walk each way from the spa to the garage. As passionate as I still was about my job, it didn't take long for a sense of routine to set in, and I started to feel this itch, this whisper, that there was something more for me to do. Nothing about my job had changed; *I* had changed. I'd been transported to the other side of life itself, and now that I'd returned, I craved something more. *Is this what the old man meant when he spoke of living differently once he returned from the other side?* There I was, standing in this quiet room every day, massaging one person after another. I'd be thinking, *I know I didn't survive in order to massage this man's hairy back.* As I listened to people's stories, I felt like I should've been out in the world, sharing my own story. I could hear an internal voice echoing: "You're meant to do so much more than this." I heard it—but I didn't really know what "more" was. And aside from that, I didn't want to get too far ahead of myself. My kidneys were still healing.

MY BROTHER-IN-LAW, JARED, called me up one afternoon in early fall 2000. "You have to turn on Blue Torch TV right now," he said, referring to the action sports network we both watched sometimes. "There's this amazing guy on here you should see." I switched on my remote and clicked through the channels to find the station. The "amazing guy" Jared had seen was Thayne Mahler, a snowboarder who, on the show that day, did a run down this mountain and then pulled up the bottom of his pants to reveal a prosthetic leg. "Oh my God!" I yelled when I saw the leg.

Right away, I went online, looked up Blue Torch, and found a phone number. A man by the name of Art answered the phone. "My name is Amy," I said, a little out of breath, "and I know this might sound like a crazy request, but you just showed a snowboarder named Thayne Mahler on your station—and I want to know what prosthetic leg he uses." "Oh, Thayne is one of my best friends," Art said. "Here's his phone number," and then he actually gave it to me. Minutes later, I was on the phone with Thayne himself. After introducing myself and telling him that I had two prosthetic legs and wanted to snowboard again, I went straight to the point: "All I really want to know is what kind of leg you use." "I use this leg that comes from a company out in Ohio," he said. "It has a shock and spring." He gave me the phone number of the company. I was beyond elated.

Thayne went on to tell me how he lost his leg. While he was snowboarding on Mount Hood in Oregon, he fell off a cliff, and his leg got wedged beneath a boulder. He was out there for a few days before he was found, and by then he'd endured extreme frostbite and his foot was broken. His leg had to be amputated below the knee. "The day I got my prosthetic leg," he told me, "I went snowboarding." I said, "You're the type of person I want to know." After asking him many more questions about snowboarding with a prosthetic (What kind of boots do you use? Do you use the pin system? How do you get up on your toes?), I thanked him for sharing so much of his time, and he graciously agreed to stay in touch with me. He even put me in touch with another snowboarder who had a prosthetic leg, Lucas, a guy who often tried to gather up adaptive snowboarders to ride together.

As soon as I finished my call with Thayne, I handwrote a letter to the company that made his athletic leg. "My name is Amy Purdy," I wrote, "and I've got two prosthetic legs. I don't know if I can ever snowboard again. But if anyone is going to do it, it's going to be me." A week after I'd mailed the letter, I received a call from the marketing director. "We'd absolutely love to work with you," she said. Within a week, I was making plans to change my socket so that this new snowboarding leg could connect to it. This seemed like the answer to my prayers. In all my searching, I never did find another snowboarder with two prosthetic legs. If no such athlete did exist, I made up my mind that I'd become the first.

THE DOCTORS GAVE my kidneys more than a year to recover. We were all hoping that since I was just nineteen when I became ill, I was young enough for my kidneys to regenerate. But by fall 2000, it was clear they weren't healing. My creatinine levels, which had been continually monitored after I left the hospital, had plateaued, signaling that my kidneys weren't recuperating; on their own, my kidneys just wouldn't be able to filter enough toxins out of my blood to keep me alive and healthy. I would need a transplant.

I'd been resisting that recommendation for months. My mom and I visited a transplant clinic one afternoon, and a nurse there told us more about the process. "After the transplant, you'll be on medication for the rest of your life," she explained. "The medica-tion can make you gain weight; sometimes people get something

called a 'moon face,' which is when your face becomes bloated."
She went on to mention other possible side effects, like the loss of
muscle mass and excessive hair in unexpected places. She also
explained that for the first six months after the surgery, patients
usually cannot work; they must carefully protect themselves from
germs; and it's recommended that they wear an antimicrobial
mask when traveling.

As the woman spoke, I was sitting there thinking, *I'm not even
the kind of person who likes to take ibuprofen, and now I may
need to be on this horrible medication forever? And I'm going to
grow hair in random parts of my body? Are you kidding me?* It
sounded like a nightmare. Carrying a dialysis machine around
everywhere I went sounded like a better idea than this. When we
finished in the clinic and went back out to the car, I turned to my
mom and exclaimed, "Hell no, I am not having a kidney transplant! It's not worth it to me." I pleaded with God, Buddha, the
Universe—any greater force that could be listening to me—to
help my kidneys recuperate.

Yet as the months passed, my blood work continued to show
my kidneys weren't recovering. I arranged to see a highly respected
kidney specialist who could give us a second opinion. After review-
ing my medical files, he made a house call to give me his assess-
ment: "Your kidneys are shot," he said. "They're not coming back.
If you're going to lead a healthy life, you need to have the transplant." In order to do the transplant, he explained, my immune
system would need to be suppressed so that my body wouldn't
fight off the new kidney. If your immune system is too strong, it
recognizes your transplanted kidney as a foreign organ, and then
it can begin to reject it.

I lost it. Once the doctor left, I went into my room and yelled and cried for an entire hour. I literally got down on my knees and shouted. Not only had I lost my legs, but now I needed a *kidney transplant?* I was just getting used to the idea of life with prosthetics, and now I'd be back in the hospital, possibly be bloated, and have a suppressed immune system my entire life!? And if I gained weight, what impact would that have on my legs—wouldn't I have to get new ones after the ones I had were finally comfortable? And what about the new snowboarding leg I'd just discovered? Would I have to delay my plan to have that leg fitted? And after finally feeling so much more independent, wouldn't this surgery put me back on the sidelines again, which would mean missing the upcoming snowboarding season? And if I needed to suppress my immune system, wouldn't that make me more susceptible to a disease like meningitis, which had wrecked my body in the first place? I felt overwhelmed with the questions, and I had no real answers for any of them.

Hearing that I'd have to have the transplant was the most frightening, most horrible news I'd ever gotten—yes, even worse than learning that I would lose my legs. Losing your legs is one thing; losing your health is another. But even still, I felt I had to go through with it. If I didn't, I'd never truly be independent again. It was a catch-22: I could either choose a life on dialysis without a new kidney to keep me healthy, or I could choose a life with immunosuppressive medication and a new kidney. I chose the latter.

Once it was settled that I was moving forward with the transplant, family, friends, and even some anonymous donors who'd heard my story in the local news stepped up. Brad's mom graciously offered her kidney, which I have always been so appreciative of. Among my family members, I really thought my sister would turn out to be a perfect candidate, given her closeness in age and optimum health. But as we went through the testing process to see who'd be the best match in terms of blood type and antigens (there are six antigens to be matched), neither Crystal nor Mom shared my blood type and enough of my antigens. My father did. Dad was almost a perfect match for me, nearly my twin. We share the same blood type and four of the six antigens.

If my father was nervous about risking his own life to save mine, he didn't show it. "Whatever you need to live a healthy, independent life," he told me, "I'm willing to give it to you." Technically, humans can survive on 10 percent of one kidney, which is why you can give one up and still live a normal life. Even still, once you're functioning on one kidney, if anything ever happened to that kidney, you'd need a transplant. That's what's most frightening about the choice to give up a healthy kidney.

The doctor at first scheduled me for the transplant on November 7. "That's my twenty-first birthday," I told him, "so we'll have to choose another date." For my landmark birthday, I wanted to go out and have fun with friends and not worry about wrecking my kidneys; after all, they were already wrecked. Because my immune system had to be crashed in order for them to do the surgery, I couldn't even have even the slightest cold or cough on the day of the operation. So I needed at least a day to let loose, and then another few days to recover from my last hurrah. They rescheduled me for November 13—exactly seven days after my birthday.

My twenty-first birthday was as much fun as I thought it would be. About thirty of my friends and family first gathered for dinner and margaritas, and from there, some of us went on to bar-hop around a few of the newer places in Vegas. By the end of the evening, it wasn't my kidneys I needed to be most worried about; it was probably my liver. Then in the days right before the surgery, I had to shift my focus from partying to preparing: When most twenty-one-year-olds are taking shots of tequila, I was taking shots of morphine and immunosuppressive medication.

By the time I entered the hospital, I'd done my best to get ready for it, and even mentally embrace the idea of receiving my new kidney. Our thoughts are powerful, and I knew that if I shifted my mind-set in this way, I would increase the chances of my body accepting the organ. The transplant was to be the first laparoscopic kidney transplant performed in Nevada. A laparoscopic transplant is a far less invasive procedure than a traditional kidney transplant: postsurgery, my dad and I would have a short hospital stay (about four days) and a faster recovery time than we would if we went with the traditional transplant operation. Because our surgeons were making medical history in Nevada, the story drew attention in the local media. On the day of the operation, the hospital brought in medical students from other states, such as California and New York; in addition, kidney specialists from all over the country flew in to witness history in the making.

I remember the day of surgery clearly. I woke up that cold November morning, looked in the mirror, and wondered, *Am I really following through with this?* I kept thinking that something might happen, last-minute, to make doctors decide they didn't need to do the transplant, that miraculously, my blood work would suddenly come back perfect, or that the surgeon would call in sick. To get myself into a relaxed state, I listened to one of the songs that often played in the spa, "So Flows the Current," by

Patrick O'Hearn. It's very mellow, which is exactly the mental space I wanted to be in.

My father went into surgery first. Before leaving, he reached over and kissed me on my forehead. "Now if you ever decide to drink alcohol again," he told me, "you're only allowed to drink the best, which is Crown Royal whiskey. That kidney is used to Crown Royal." We both chuckled. "I love you, Dad," I said. I could feel a tear slowly rolling down my right cheek. "And thank you." We were both very emotional, but you can imagine how tearful and nerve-racking this was for my poor mom. Two of the people she loved most were about to simultaneously undergo a risky procedure. She handled it all with such grace.

They wheeled my dad into the operating room. As soon as they took my father back, I put on my headphones to listen to more mellow music and to keep myself as relaxed as possible. That didn't last long: I began to panic, so the nurses knocked me out with some sort of medication.

Once my father's procedure was under way, the surgeon nearly had to call it off. He realized that instead of having one large artery leading to his kidneys, my father had three, and that can lead to complications such as major blood loss. My father's extra arteries hadn't shown up on the X-rays and MRIs the doctor had done beforehand. Normally, when such a discovery is made, many surgeons discontinue the operation and sew up the patient. But our doctor opted to go through with the operation because he was confident that he could complete it successfully, especially with some of the best transplant doctors in the country right there with him. He also felt it was a great opportunity to show the students who'd gathered how to handle a high-risk transplant. So he

I've always loved this photo because it reminds me of how carefree I was as a child. Little did I know what was in store for my life. I was born with blond hair, and then it turned strawberry blond, and then finally brown.

Three years old, wearing my favorite overalls in the back of my dad's truck. I loved being outside, and playing in my dad's truck is one of my clearest memories from when I was little.

My sister, Crystal, and me in our cowgirl dresses, getting ready to go to the Helldorado rodeo. Attending the annual rodeo was my family's tradition even before my dad worked there.

Fishing with my grandpa and my mom. To this day, we still go to Utah every summer and make sure to fish with my grandpa.

Going camping with my Grandma and Grandpa Campbell, my sister, and my cousins. We loved camping in Utah! It was one of our favorite things to do in the summer.

I always enjoyed the snow, but I was never really a good skier. I snowplowed the majority of the time and couldn't stand having cold feet. However, I loved the outdoors and always looked forward to our family trips.

With my first snowboard, a Gnu skidder. It was love at first ride!

At fifteen, I stood with my first snowboard. I was wearing my friend Josh's pants and a big hoodie, since I hadn't yet bought any snowboard clothing of my own!

In this picture, taken one morning before my sister, Crystal, and I drove off to school in the beat-up red Chevy we shared, I am a sophomore and she is a senior. Crystal was not only the head varsity cheerleader, she was and still is my biggest fan, an amazing role model, and the best sister I could ever ask for.

1998, all dressed up and heading to my senior prom.

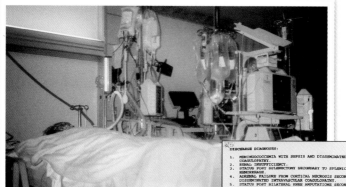

Just twenty-four hours after entering the hospital. My mom took this photo after I was put into an induced coma. She thought, *If Amy survives this, she will never believe what she went through.*

Here is a summary of my stay in the hospital from my doctor. It explains the bleak condition I was in when entering the hospital, as well as what I endured during my stay.

With Dr. Abby after I awakened from my coma. He visited my bedside every day while I was in the hospital. We are still great friends, and I credit him and his intuition for playing a huge part in my survival.

Just days after getting my new legs, I stood up and danced with my dad. It's interesting to think that my life has come full circle. In this moment, who would have known that I would eventually go on to compete on *Dancing with the Stars*?

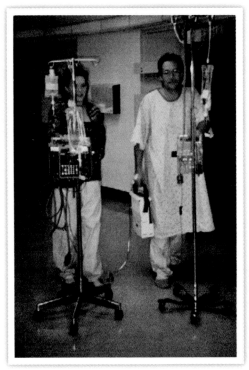

My dad and I walk down the hospital halls the morning after our kidney transplant. They had us up on our feet in no time! I couldn't be more grateful for his gift.

My friend Johnny walked me down the aisle at my sister's wedding. This is when I learned how much we can accomplish if we are determined enough. I took my first steps toward a new life.

Just a few months after leaving the hospital, I weighed just under ninety pounds. Here I am with my little Roxy baby, my little angel in fur. As challenging as it was that she ran away daily, she was the best physical therapy I could have had. She walked by my side through one of the most difficult chapters of my life.

Putting shoes on the feet of South African children during the Toms/ Element Skateboards Shoe Drop. This was one of the most fulfilling experiences of my life. The children had very little, yet they were so full of love and gratitude. *(Photo courtesy Marc Falkenstien.)*

Here I am trying on the legs Nikki Sixx had made for our photo shoot. These legs made me feel extremely feminine—I loved how long, lean, and pointed they were, like the ultimate stiletto! Believe it or not, I could balance and walk on them.

Testing out my new snowboard feet in a lab in Colorado. I'm always trying to up my game!

Me and Daniel in front of our house in Lake Tahoe, California. It has been amazing to share a passion and work together with him on Adaptive Action Sports. "Live Beyond Limits" became the motto of our organization and also my personal mantra.

Giving my TED Talk at TEDx Orange Coast. This was one of the scariest yet most powerful moments of my life. Speaking at TED launched an international professional speaking career for me, and I learned how much you can grow when you step outside of your comfort zone. *(Photo courtesy Barbara S. Giordano.)*

In 2012, my sister remarried (her second husband is Troy Norris), and this is our beautiful family. From the left top: Aunt Debbie, Aunt Cindy, Grandpa and Grandma Campbell, mom, dad, me, and Daniel. From the left bottom: Troy, Danny (my cousin Michelle's little boy), my sister, Crystal, her children, Bryten and Jonas, and Troy's daughters, Bree and Acey. *(Photo courtesy Deena Antonucci Photography.)*

In this photo, I was testing out my feet on Copper Mountain. My goal was to always be able to get as much ankle flexion and knee bend as possible so that I'd have clean, fast carves, which are needed for boardercross.

The view out of the start gate of the Sochi Olympic race course. The snow was so inconsistent and bumpy that my goal was just to stay stable on my feet.

Winning the bronze at the 2014 Paralympic Games in Sochi! I was so grateful to even be on the podium. It's difficult for me to explain the feeling of having my hard work pay off. I was so thankful that I could bring a medal home for all who supported me, and for my country. It still makes me emotional to think about it. If something doesn't exist, we have the power to create it! *(Photo courtesy The Hartford Financial Services Group, Inc. Photographer Joe Kusumoto.)*

Just ten hours after arriving in Los Angeles from Sochi, Russia, my dance partner, Derek Hough and I had our official photo shoot for Season 18 of *Dancing with the Stars*. The whole experience was so surreal—I couldn't believe I was actually on the show!

I walked through a door in the rehearsal studio, and it led to this sparkly magical kingdom of past *DWTS* costumes—a girl's dream closet come true!

Derek and I work on my feet, which was a daily thing in our rehearsals. We would try out different feet and see what movements we could accomplish with them. No matter how hard things got, we always found a way to make the dance work.

Here Derek and I are developing ideas for our finale freestyle dance, which I did up on my tippy toes in these special swimming feet. After balancing on those feet throughout the season, my core was so strong!

OPRAH

May 13, 2014

Amy,

Congratulations on making it to the finals!
Looking forward to our dinner.

Oprah

The note that Oprah sent to me (along with the most gorgeous flowers!) when Derek and I made it to the *DWTS* finale.

Derek and I try out the aerial move for our final dance. Thank goodness I was in shape! Holding your body weight by one hand while spinning is not an easy feat! That move ended up being a powerful finale statement. Derek is brilliant!

I never considered myself an athlete until just a few years ago, however I've always taken to sports pretty easily. I grew up water skiing and wakeboarding with my family on the lake, and I still love it to this day. I pretty much set my feet up the same way I do for snowboarding.

Me and my mom on her sixtieth birthday! My mom is a Christmas baby—she was born on Christmas Eve, and I can only pray that I have her genes and look as good as she does when I'm her age! To me she has always been the most beautiful, loving, nurturing woman I have ever known. I still hope to grow up to be like my mom one day.

Me and Oprah in Atlanta during the "Life You Want" Tour. It was so surreal to walk out on stage with her! I used to look to the stories she'd share for inspiration, and there I was standing with her, sharing my own story with the world. Amazing. *(Copyright © Harpo Studios, Inc. George Burns, photographer.)*

On the red carpet at the 2014 ESPY Awards! My inspiration for this outfit was to play on the bionic look of my leg. This photo was taken exactly fifteen years to the day after I entered the hospital, the fifteen-year anniversary of when my life changed forever. What an incredible full-circle moment.

proceeded, and because he had to do so with such caution, the surgery lasted for six hours. Once they'd removed the kidney from my dad, the doctors wheeled me to his side and transplanted the kidney. They didn't remove either of my two kidneys; they just gave me a third one.

My next memory was waking up the following morning in a hospital room. "How's Dad?" I said sleepily to my mom. I looked down to see the bandages across my stomach, then back at her. "He made it through just fine," she reassured me. "You both did. He's over in the next room." Though the operation had gone well, my father was in incredible pain because of a postsurgery procedure that involved filling his abdominal cavity with air. That procedure was more uncomfortable than the surgery or incision, and it was hard to see my dad in so much pain.

As for me, I woke up feeling like a million bucks! I didn't realize just how sick I'd been until I woke up feeling so healthy. Yes, there were some side effects from the postsurgery medication I was given: My hands were somewhat shaky, and I did experience hot flashes. But my overwhelming feeling was one of gratitude. For my dad. For my mom. For my life.

My father gave me life twice: the first time when I was born, and the second time when he offered me his kidney. It will forever be the best birthday gift I receive. How do you even begin to thank someone for such a profound gift? How do you show someone how appreciative you are? You do it not just in words, but in the way you choose to live—as fully, as bravely, and as richly as possible. And that was what I was going to do.

I really don't know all that went through my father's head at the time that he was preparing to give me one of his kidneys. He never expressed the concern that he no doubt had to be feeling. He just proudly stepped forward and offered to put his life on the line in order to save his daughter's. I can only hope that the courage my father displayed, the courage that emboldened him to give me such an invaluable gift, is the same courage I can show during my own journey. Thank you, Dad.

CHAPTER 11

Connection

"Being deeply loved by someone gives you strength,
while loving someone deeply gives you courage."
—LAO-TZU

I did have a slight moon face after the kidney transplant. But because I was feeling so much better overall by then, it didn't bother me. Yes, I did endure a lot of poking and prodding; the doctors had to adjust my medications to relieve tremors; I spent a lot of time indoors to limit my exposure to germs; and I had to take thirty pills a day. Yet there were also some pleasant surprises. Instead of growing a lot of unwanted hair as a side effect of the medication, I actually grew more of the hair I *did* want. My red-brown mane became very thick, and my eyelashes had never been so full. And the best news was that I didn't have a single rejection episode. By three months after the surgery, both my dad and I were feeling fine. Even great.

One evening in late January 2001, Thayne Mahler, the snow-boarder I connected with after I saw him on TV, called me up.

"A few of us snowboarders are meeting up in Mammoth Mountain to do a competition," he said, explaining that the United States of America Snowboard Association (USASA) was holding its national event there. "You should come up."

I paused. "I don't even know if I can snowboard," I said. "I tried once last year, and it was rough. I've got this new snowboard leg, but I haven't even had a chance to test it, because I had this kidney surgery."

"Well, think about it," he said. "It would be great if you could come up." A couple of weeks later, Lucas also called me. After Thayne had connected us, we'd chatted a few times. "You really should come up to Mammoth," he said.

"Well, I don't know. I may not be ready."

"Just come," he urged. "You won't be sorry."

Mammoth Mountain, in Northern California, is only about a five-hour drive from Las Vegas, so I began thinking, *Maybe I could just meet them up there. It might be fun. I don't have to do the competition. I could just go up and try out the new leg.* "Mom, will you drive with me?" I asked her one afternoon. "Absolutely," she said. So the following weekend, we loaded into the SUV and headed for Mammoth. Once there, we checked into a hotel for the weekend.

I immediately felt like I fit in with these guys. Not only did I meet Thayne and Lucas for the first time in person; I also met the five other snowboarders who'd traveled there for the competition. These were my kind of people: They were all just as passionate as I was about riding, so interested in comparing notes about what worked with their legs and what didn't work. None of them had two prosthetic legs, like me, but they all had the same spirit of adventure. "Amy, I'm so glad you came up," Lucas said, greeting me warmly with a high-five. "This is going to be fun."

And it was. Over the next three days on my new athletic leg, I snowboarded nonstop—without nearly the same struggles that I had in Lee Canyon. Between runs, I traded ideas with the other snowboarders on everything from finding the right boots to the best way to carve and how to get up on your toes. As for the new athletic legs, they didn't turn out to be the greatest. They were too bouncy, and every time I hit a bump, they were overresponsive. Even still, they did outdo those beginner legs. And at least these new legs had a bit more foot flexion and built-in shocks, which made maneuvering far easier. So it was an improvement. Not perfection by any means, but progress.

On day three, I surprised myself when I did the unexpected: I signed up to race in the USASA national amateur competition. Riding for those days leading up to the competition—and then getting better at it with each run—had boosted my confidence and shown me how physically capable I was. I'd underestimated myself. "You should try the competition, Amy," my mom had said all weekend, encouraging me. "You might be better than you think."

My mother was right: In my first snowboard competition after losing my legs, I earned three bronze medals. And more important, I sent a clear and powerful message to myself that the dreams I envisioned could actually become real. Three months before, I'd been lying on a surgery table, and thanks to the encouragement of some newfound friends, I'd found my way from that table and up to the top of a snowcapped mountain. If that was possible, anything was—and is.

. . .

JUST A FEW months after my transplant, I went back to work—same job, same amazing Canyon Ranch managers who again held my position open for me. I worked part-time for the spa, and I took a side job in a chiropractor's office. That summer, I also enrolled in an aesthetics program. I'd always loved to do makeup (it's like painting—so it appeals to the artist in me), and I wanted to learn more about skin care. I also realized that, as much as I loved my job as a massage therapist, it could become increasingly difficult for me to stay on my feet for hours at a time. If, in addition to massage, I could also do facials and makeup, that would be easier on my legs. I applied, and by November 2001, I'd completed the program.

About a year after the Mammoth competition, I reconnected with Lucas. "Some of us are meeting up in Crested Butte, Colorado, to snowboard," he said. "You should come. We're meeting some others there who are also getting back into snowboarding." When I Googled "Crested Butte," it looked like a breathtakingly beautiful, quaint town with a great local community. The main street was bordered by colorful buildings; bars and restaurants lined the narrow streets; there were outdoor music festivals. It was the kind of place I'd dreamed of calling home, a town where I could enjoy the crisp mountain air and snowboard as often as I wanted. "Okay, I'll meet you guys up there," I told Lucas—and a couple of weeks later, I did. Our plan was to get a condo that several of us could share and then to snowboard for a few days.

One evening, our group went out to a bar called the Black Whale. Across the bar, I noticed this really hot guy—tan skin, dark hair, chiseled cheekbones, and the most beautiful smile I'd ever seen. He was playing pool. I could tell by the way he was dressed that he was without a doubt a skater: jeans, skate shirt,

Vans. All night, he kept smiling at me. We caught eyes a few times, then he'd look away, then he'd look over at me again. He was so attractive that I thought he was probably smiling at girls other than just me. So I resisted meeting eyes again or talking with him; plus, I was only passing through town.

The following day was Super Bowl Sunday. So to watch the big game, my friends and I went to Rafters, a massive sports bar with pool tables and big-screen TVs. The place was packed. I shared a table with my group and some others we'd met up there—there was one kid in a wheelchair and a lady who was visually impaired. At one point, I got up to walk her to the bathroom, and when I walked back again, I saw the same hot guy. He smiled. It seemed as if he'd positioned himself so that he could see me from where he was seated. Amid the shouts of those enjoying the game, this guy got up and came over to our table.

"Hello," he said, extending his hand to the kid in the wheel-chair. "I'm Daniel." He then went around the entire circle and introduced himself to every person at the table. I was impressed, because it's not easy to just walk up to a table and connect with a group of strangers. When he got to me, I told him my name. He smiled.

"Would you like to play a game of pool?" he asked.

"Sure," I said, blushing a little. "I'd be happy to play."

For the rest of the evening, we played pool, had some drinks, and chatted about snowboarding. He was currently in school, working toward a degree in resort management and recreation. "It's great up here," he said. "Every chance I get, I'm snowboarding." After even just the first few minutes of hanging with him, I realized how down-to-earth he was. He was a genuinely nice guy, one who probably had no idea I had on two prosthetic legs. I noticed that he had the same skateboard shoe company logo on his hat that I had on my legs. Just for fun one night, I'd slapped the stickers on my legs. I saw that as an opportunity to let Daniel know what he was dealing with right from the start. "Hey look, we're twins," I said, lifting my pant leg so he could see the sticker. He didn't blink or have a crazy reaction. He just grinned. "Whoa, that's cool," he said. "Well," I continued, "I have two." I then pulled up the other pant leg. "Okay, now that's really cool," he said. Then without missing a beat, he asked: "Do you want to snowboard tomorrow?" "Sure," I said.

The following afternoon at one, we met at the half-pipe. When I arrived, I saw this guy doing 360s and 540s out of the pipe, then I realized it was him. Not only was he hot—he was clearly also a brilliant snowboarder. When he saw me, he rode over.

"That was amazing," I said. He smiled wide, that same megawatt grin he'd flashed in the bar.

"Well, thanks," he said. "Wanna give it a shot?"

"Sure," I said.

Over the next hour, I didn't quite keep up with Daniel, but we did have a lot of fun. I'd learned to carve my way down the mountain so well by then that if you didn't know I had prosthetics, you wouldn't.

"You're good!" Daniel said. Given how accomplished of a snowboarder he was, I knew he was being generous, but I accepted the compliment. I had improved, even since Mammoth.

That evening, Daniel came back to the condo with me. The guys were there, and so was one of the kids who was in a wheelchair. The wheel on his chair was coming loose. "Do you mind if I take a quick look at it?" Daniel asked. The kid nodded and Daniel sat down next to the chair. I was impressed for the second time with Daniel. *This guy isn't afraid to jump right in and help people.* He fixed the chair, and he seemed totally at ease.

That evening, we stayed up late talking and learning more about each other. I told him all about my family, growing up in Vegas, and all the adventures I still wanted to have. He listened intently, then shared more about his background and travels: He'd studied in Spain, he'd lived in Hawaii for a time, and he and his mom had once spent several months camping out in Puerto Vallarta, Mexico. *Such a worldly guy.* He'd also worked as an adventure tour guide for a travel tour company, which meant he'd guided tourists across the United States and Canada; he'd been to every single state in the United States. "We skydived, rock-climbed, scuba dived—you name it," he said. "Meeting people from all over the world was great."

His parents, who'd adopted him, had raised him to love travel, and they visited countries all around the world. His father had mostly worked in government (Daniel grew up in the Washington, D.C., area), and on the side, his dad piloted his own plane; his mother was the first female firefighter in Montana. His mom also worked as a grant writer, trying to secure funding for Native American tribes. When Daniel was just eleven, he lost his dad in a plane crash. In the face of that devastation, Daniel's mother bravely carried on with raising Daniel and his older brother, who was also adopted, though Daniel and his brother have different birth parents.

I was absolutely fascinated by the fact that his family was so different from mine. Their entire lifestyle was built around exploring different cultures, whereas I grew up in what felt like an all-American bubble. And not only were Daniel and his brother adopted (Daniel is a mix of Spanish and Native American, which is where his gorgeous dark skin comes from), but so were some of his cousins. "I'd love to get out and live somewhere different again," Daniel told me as our evening together came to a close. Like me, he'd dreamed of living in all kinds of places—and he wanted to see more of the world.

The following day, Daniel had classes and I went snowboarding again—so we didn't see each other. But he was definitely on my mind. Here was the kind of guy who had been to so many places, he was four years older than I was, and could teach me a lot—nothing like some of the guys I'd dated who'd never even left Vegas. I was hungry for knowledge of the outside world, and Daniel was someone who could share it with me.

That evening, my last in Crested Butte, he met up with me and my friends in the same bar we'd been in the night before. Later that evening, once I was back at the condo, he called. "I'd like to see you again before you fly out," he said. "I leave first thing in the morning," I told him. "Can I take you to the airport in the morning?" he asked. "It's pretty early," I said. "My flight's at seven, so I'd have to leave here by five." "That's okay," he said. "I'd like to pick you up." "Well, okay," I said. "Then I'll see you bright and early."

Just before five, he pulled up to our condo in his Bronco. When I saw the Bronco, my mind flashed back to my high school days, riding up to the mountains in Aaron's Bronco. "How are you this morning?" he asked. "Good," I said. Over the next forty-five minutes, he drove us along the winding roads of the mountainside and we watched the beautiful sunrise as we chatted. I was in heaven. "I'd love to stay in touch with you," he said as we pulled into the airport. "Definitely," I said with a smile, but not overdoing it because I still wasn't sure where this could go. "Okay, so I have your number and I'll give you a call," he said. We hugged and I headed off to make my flight.

A few months after we'd been talking, we had definitely fallen for one another. I began visiting Daniel in Crested Butte every few weeks. I loved being up in the mountains, and I also loved his group of friends, all of whom seemed as carefree as Daniel. In Vegas, my life was all about work and doctors; though I was feeling great, I still had plenty of appointments. On those weekends when I traveled to meet Daniel in Crested Butte, I could get away from it all and clear my head. It felt like a little vacation from the responsibilities of my life at home. And in between my visits, Daniel and I talked daily. We might not have been calling it a serious romance at that point, but it was. And though I'll fade to black on the details of our intimacy, there were plenty of fireworks, trust me. What made it even more special was the fact that he completely put me at ease. Never once did I feel awkward about revealing my body, my scars, or my legs. Daniel has always said that my legs didn't bother him. The day he noticed me in the bar, he says he just noticed a hot chick with a nice butt, and that's all he saw!

A few months after we met, Daniel and I traveled together to Washington, D.C., so I could meet his family. Right away, I fell in love with Daniel's mother—so warm, friendly, and interested in the lives of people around her. Her door was always open to anyone who needed a place to stay.

Once I was back in Vegas and Daniel returned to Colorado, we continued to see one another, just not as frequently because I became busier with work. We still talked all the time and visited each other as much as we could, but a month and a half or more could go by between our visits. Even with the distance between us, we'd absolutely become best friends. Up to then, I'd floated from one relationship to the next, never lingering for very long, but whenever I was with Daniel, this butterfly wanted to land and stay around.

Back when I'd completed my program and become a licensed aesthetician, I'd started thinking about moving out of Vegas again. I felt strong enough. My legs were feeling great and fitting well. I was becoming more independent. And I was ready to take the next step toward more freedom, toward exploring the many items on my bucket list. I was continuously aware that I'd been given a second chance at life—and I chose to stay—so I intended to pack in as much excitement on my journey as I could. And I kept remembering that voice, that intuitive sense I felt that compelled me to do something different.

I had a new idea for every minute of the day. I yearned for some kind of creative outlet, some form of artistic expression. I thought about moving to Los Angeles to try acting. My friend Beth had eventually left Vegas and moved to L.A. to pursue an acting career there. I also loved fashion and thought, *Wouldn't it be cool to open up a magazine and see this beautiful model, and then later find out that she had a prosthetic leg?* And when it came to changing cities, I dreamed about living close to the ocean.

"I'd love to move to a beach town," I told Daniel one evening. "Like San Diego."

At the time, Daniel was still finishing up his program in Colorado, but he'd been considering taking a break from school.

"We could both move there," he said. "We could get a place on the beach."

"Really?" I said.

"Sure," he said. "It'll be fun." Within a few weeks of that conversation, we'd agreed to move.

Daniel relocated to San Diego first in early 2003. He got an apartment right on the beach with a friend and began working as a surf instructor. As much as I'd been eager to leave Vegas, I didn't want to make my leap too quickly. My job had such a flexible schedule and I made great money, so I thought, *Why not live between the two cities for a while and get all the benefits of both?* So about a month after Daniel moved, I joined him in San Diego, I'd spend two weeks with him there, then two weeks back in Vegas. I've always loved to drive and I actually looked forward to the five-and-a-half-hour car trips. For several months, I lived that way.

BY SPRING 2003, I was ready to join Daniel full-time in San Diego. Just as I began making plans for that transition, I got the kind of call you don't get every day. It was from Madonna's manager.

"Hello, is this Amy Purdy?"

"Yes it is." I sat down on the sofa.

"Hello, Amy," she said. "I'm Madonna's manager. We're doing a music video in L.A., and Madonna wants to feature a young woman who can play a runway model and who also has prosthetic legs. We heard about you, and I wanted to know if you could come out and be in the video."

I nearly dropped the phone. "Uh, yes," I said, my voice tremoring. "When is it?"

"It's in two days."

While I picked up my jaw from the ground, the woman went

on to explain that she'd gotten my phone number from an actor she'd previously worked with, a man I'd met the summer before through the San Diego organization called Challenged Athletes Foundation (CAF). Little had I known that by meeting him, I'd one day be getting a call from one of my musical idols.

"Can we fly you out to L.A. this Wednesday?" the manager pressed, trying to pull me out of my state of speechlessness.

"Oh my gosh, yes," I said. "I can!"

"The video is for the song 'American Life,'" she told me.

This was exactly the kind of thing I'd wanted to do. And leave it to Madonna, the forward-thinking artist who'd once been the inspiration for me to chop off my Barbie dolls' hair, to create such a unique video. How amazing would it be for the world to see a video that made prosthetic legs actually look cool? As soon as I put down the phone, my mind raced with what I needed to do to get ready: *How will I wear my hair? What should I wear? Which feet should I pack? And will I get to meet the Material Girl herself?*

I drove out to Los Angeles and stayed with Beth and her boyfriend—by this time she was dating actor Jason Lee. From their gorgeous home, I drove myself to the studio. When I arrived, the building was abuzz: The cast and crew busied themselves around the set, preparing for the shoot. I was ushered backstage to meet with the wardrobe team. "We're not sure what to put you in," said the wardrobe manager. She wandered off, rifling through the massive racks of clothes. She returned a few minutes later holding a beige peasant-looking dress; it was one of the most drab outfits I'd ever seen. "Let's put you in this," she said, holding it up. I ducked away to a dressing room, removed my jeans and shirt, and put on the dress. The dress draped down to the floor, covering my legs, and I kept thinking, *If the point was for me to show my legs, then why did they even hire me if they were planning to cover me up?*

A few minutes later, someone shuffled me over to the hair and makeup area—and the stylist put my hair in these two big braids. Not what I was expecting: I looked like an orphaned Princess Leah! Before a few other girls and I were ushered to the set, a stage manager collected our phones. "There are to be no photos taken of the video set," she explained. She finally led us into the studio, this cavernous, warehouse-like room in which a long runway and scores of stage lights were set up. The song "American Life" suddenly began blasting over the loudspeakers.

"Okay," said the manager, "in a few minutes, I want you to go out there and strut down the runway, turn around at the end, and then walk back. Do you know how to do a runway walk?"

"Kind of," I said. I didn't really, but I'd seen enough models in all the fashion magazines I'd looked through to figure out how to pull it off.

I put on my best model face (focused, brave, confident) and strutted out to the amazing beat of the song carrying me. When I got to the end, there sat Madonna in a director's chair. Right then, I got an idea: I pulled up the lower edge of my dress so she could see my legs. I figured if I'd been hired for my legs, she should at least get a look at them. I then did a little sassy dance move, turned around, and—with an attitude—strutted off. The moment I got backstage, I heard her yell, "Cut!" The music stopped.

Madonna came running backstage. "Hello, I'm Madonna," she said, looking directly at me. I was thinking, *I know.* She looked so much more petite in person than I'd imagined she'd be. "You are absolutely beautiful!" she told me.

"Thank you," I said, blushing. I hadn't truly expected to meet her that day, so I hadn't been nervous, but once I was actually standing backstage talking to her, I did feel my heart flutter. She had exactly the natural aura of confidence and power that I would've expected her to have.

"Do you mind if I sex you up?"

I shook my head, not quite sure what was coming next—but wanting to find out. "You're Madonna," I told her. "You can do whatever you want to me." She laughed a little.

"Okay, take this dress off," she said. Right there in front of everyone, I lifted off my dress and stood there in just my underwear and metal legs. She grabbed a pair of camo boy shorts.

"Do you mind being a bit exposed? Because I love this scar down your stomach." She looked down toward my belly button.

"No," I said.

"Okay, then put these on," she said, handing me the shorts. I bent down to step into them. I loved the way she talked. She had such a clear idea of what she wanted.

Next, Madonna had one of the stylists place duct tape in the shape of an X across each one of my breasts. A fur wrap topped off my new look. I couldn't really wear super-tall heels, but I happened to bring black platform wedge shoes that worked with the outfit. Before leaving backstage, Madonna handed me off to the designer Jeremy Scott, and I knew exactly who he was from all the fashion magazines I'd read. He spent the next hour showing me how to do a proper runway catwalk (and by the way, the key is to keep your chin up, throw your shoulders down and back, push your hips slightly forward, put one foot right in front of the other, and balance most of your weight on your toe rather than on your heel—tough to do, and even tougher in prosthetics and wedges). Good thing that when I got my new legs, I practiced balancing and walking on the curbs down my street, one foot in front of the other. "Just visualize Giselle strutting down the Victoria's Secret catwalk with an attitude," Jeremy coached. "Remember to move with the music!" Then when I reached the end of the runway, he told me, I was to throw open my fur and do a little booty-shake dance. I practiced the walk five or six times, and by the end, I had it down pretty well.

Once we were done, Jeremy took me over to hair and makeup. A half hour later, I emerged, bronzed from head to toe. My hair was completely wild, all over my head. I had dark, edgy eye makeup.

Before I went back out onto the set, a manager explained the idea of the video—which was to be, among many other things, Madonna's artistic statement about the atrocities of war, along with themes of the fashion industry's narrow depiction of beauty. The whole video was to be Madonna's view on what American life, hence the title, had evolved into. In one portion of the video (the segment I was to appear in), a parade of seemingly similar runway models would be shown from the waist up, but then when the camera panned out, it would reveal that I, unlike the other models, had metal legs. "Give it everything you've got when you go out there," she told me, and a few minutes later, I did exactly that. I strutted out confidently, kept my head up high, and then when I got to the end of the runway, I did a better version of my little booty dance than I'd even done in practice. Jeremy, who was watching from the sideline, gave me a thumbs-up. *I did it.*

After my part of the performance was finished, I asked to sit next to Madonna, who was back in her director's chair. I hung out with her for the entire rest of the day. We didn't really talk much, but it was a thrill just to sit there and take it all in. I loved the whole energy of the scene: the million-dollar set, the half-naked runway models all over the place, the infectious music, the flashing lights, the cameras everywhere. I found it all exhilarating! What a dream to be part of such an amazing production—to be introduced to yet another world I knew little about. And to think that just a few short years before, I'd been lying in the ICU, battling for my every breath. Before I left, one of the camera guys I'd chatted with came backstage and gave me a little black-and-white photo of myself on the catwalk. "You're never going to forget this moment," he said. He was right: I will forever keep that photo—along with my memory of the day.

The video never aired. At the time of its scheduled worldwide release, President George W. Bush officially declared war on Iraq, and Madonna released a statement explaining that in light of the country's invasion of Iraq, she didn't want to release a video that could be construed as antimilitary or anti-American. Even though I never got to see the video, the whole experience was completely empowering for me. I became even more interested in working in Hollywood someday, whether that was behind the camera or in front of it.

I WAS READY for my complete move to San Diego. I longed to be with Daniel full-time. So a few weeks after the Madonna video, I put in a final notice at my job in Vegas. I'd already found a new position in a San Diego spa, a place where I could do makeup, skin care, and massage. Perfect.

My move was a big deal for my family, especially for my mom, who'd cared for me in all those months right after both surgeries. "Are you sure you'll be okay?" my mother would ask. My mom wasn't trying to hold me back. She was just expressing her motherly concern for my well-being. I think it helped that I'd eased into the change—by this time, my family had gotten used to me being away for two weeks at a time. They also liked Daniel, especially since they could see how much we enjoyed each other and how tender and caring he was with me. "I'll be fine," I reassured both my parents. And I knew that if I needed to return, I was less than a day's drive from Vegas.

My dad helped me load up my furniture, and he and my mom drove with me out to San Diego. My sweet Roxy had to stay because dogs weren't allowed in our house. I think the transition was harder for my parents than it was for me. They'd completely taken me under their wing and organized their lives so they could look after me, and when you do that, letting go is understandably difficult. And after all, my father wasn't just dropping off any daughter; he was dropping off the one who was carrying his kidney. Daniel and I got our own place, a tiny, four-hundred-square-foot bungalow right on Ocean Beach, for eight hundred dollars per month. My parents took me there and we said our goodbyes.

As much as I enjoyed San Diego and being there with Daniel, the transition had its challenges. San Diego is a party town, especially on the beach, and Daniel and his friends were part of it. I enjoyed it, too, but the reality was that I couldnt let myself go wild. I had this new organ inside me that I always had to think about, in the same way that an expectant mother would have to think about her unborn child. It forced me to grow up quicker than I might have otherwise, because I had the responsibility of staying healthy.

It was difficult. We'd be in a bar, somebody would order a whole round of shots for everyone, and it was like, "Woo-hoo, let's party!" I was the one who often had to abstain. I felt like the permanent designated driver. They could all stay out until three in the morning without a care in the world. But I couldn't do that. I had major cares, and my kidney was one of them. At times, I did indulge myself with the drinking and stay out all night, but I never felt good about it in the morning. Here I had this amazing kidney, this gift, and I felt guilty when I didn't take care of it. And when it came to socializing, it didn't help matters that I'm allergic to shellfish, and San Diego is *filled* with shellfish! I can't tell you how many times I'd be out with friends and have to pass on the shrimp cocktails. I tried to take everything in stride, reminding myself how grateful I was for my life and health. But to be honest, it was hard for me to be so young and not to be able to fully participate, because I really *wanted* to.

Daniel was very supportive, but he loved to party as much as I did, and I always hated to cut his fun short. And besides that, I've always admired how social Daniel is, how great he is at bringing people together. I wanted him to enjoy that.

"I'm sorry I'm not one of those girls who can go out and drink with you every night," I'd sometimes tell Daniel.

"It's okay," he always told me. "It doesn't matter to me." But it did matter to me. This Vegas girl likes to party.

There was also the entire party beach town scene to get used to—gorgeous girls everywhere, walking around in bikinis, some of them flirting with Daniel. I'd come a long way in accepting my body, but at times I did battle with insecurity. Many of my scars were still quite visible. When I got dressed in the mornings, I couldn't just throw on a dress and flip-flops and run out the door. I always had to think about how my legs would look in whatever I was wearing. The days of carefree dressing were gone.

As much as I battled with myself about the issue, I did have a small breakthrough one evening. I was lying in bed, totally naked and without my legs. I looked at my whole body in a nearby mirror—and in that moment, I became very aware that this body, scars and all, had actually saved me. It had pulled me through some gnarly-ass shit. It was strong. I had worked it out like hell, so I was healthy and in great shape. In that sense, it was beautiful. I just had to force myself to remember that during moments of insecurity.

San Diego wasn't all allergies, body issues, and tequila abstinence: There were definitely things about my time there that I loved, like the weather, the smell of the ocean, and waking up to the sound of the waves crashing against the sand. The first time I stepped foot on the sand, I realized just how much I missed the sand between my toes and the cool ocean breeze on my legs. But the minute that thought would enter my mind, I would remind myself that I most likely wouldn't have been there had I not lost my legs. I also loved my work. As usual, I threw myself into it 100 percent, and after a massage or facial, I was always happy to hear one of my clients say, "That was the best treatment I've ever had." I lived for that sentence. It felt good to be able to offer a great service and to have people actually appreciate it.

When we weren't working, Daniel and I spent a lot of time in the evenings just walking along the beach, riding our bikes or going out to listen to a live band. There were some great up-and-coming bands passing through San Diego. I didn't really get into the ocean very much. But I still loved being outdoors and staying active, and a few months after I got to San Diego, I even decided to relearn how to skateboard, and since Daniel is a big skateboarder, I wanted us to be able to skate together. But each time I got on the board, I wobbled all over the place. With snowboarding your feet attach to the board, so when you move, the board moves. That is not the case, of course, with skateboarding.

"How about if you let me drill a hole in your skateboard," suggested Daniel. Later, after he'd returned from a trip to the hardware store, he drilled a hole into the front of the board and attached a pole I could hold on to for balance. I loved the way he seemed to always have a creative solution. That's one of the many things that have always attracted me to Daniel. Many evenings we would skate down to Main Street to have dinner at our favorite fish taco spot. That's the kind of simple existence Daniel and I shared in San Diego: the pleasure of watching the sunset over the ocean, the smell of salt water in the air, the sound of the ocean waves. I'd spent most of my life in a desert just three hundred miles northeast of there—a mere five hours' drive away, yet an altogether different world.

CHAPTER 12

Action Plan

"None of us will ever accomplish anything excellent or commanding except when he listens to the whisper which is heard by him alone."
—RALPH WALDO EMERSON

There's something I've always loved about my relationship with Daniel: We're both creative. We constantly bounce ideas off one another. As our connection grew over our first two years in San Diego, so did our desire to find a way to help others. I was hearing that whisper again, that feeling that I'd been given a choice to return to life so that I could do something more purposeful. We didn't know exactly what we'd do; we only knew that once we had the right idea, we would somehow find a way. One evening in late 2004, Daniel and I had this conversation, a version of which we'd had many times:

"After getting sick, I learned how to snowboard and skateboard again on my own," I said. "But what's out there for others who have prosthetic legs and who want to get into action sports? What are their resources?"

"There are none," said Daniel, reminding me of all the searching I'd done. "But how about if we *create* something, a way for adaptive athletes to at least get in touch with one another?"

"We could start some kind of online forum," I said.

"Or a website," he added.

"Or we could do some kind of business." We both nodded.

Daniel was right: When I'd scoured the Internet, I found zero resources. There was a lot of information about how those with physical challenges could get into the classic sports, like swimming, cycling, and running; Challenged Athletes Foundation (CAF) had that covered. But there was nothing available for those who, like me, wanted to get into action sports—or who simply wanted to connect and share ideas on things like finding the best snowboarding legs. In Google, I'd put in search terms such as "amputee snowboarder," "disabled snowboarder," and "prosthetic snowboarder." I could never find a community. So one day when we were talking about our evolving idea with Daniel's mom, Nancy, whose career is philanthropy, she said, "You guys should start a nonprofit." Daniel and I got really excited about that idea, excited enough to sign up for a Learning Annex course about how to start a nonprofit.

The class was packed. "I want to go around the room and have each of you share your idea for your organization," said the instructor.

One at a time, people presented their ideas, and some said things like "I want to save the world."

"Well, but how?" asked the teacher. "You need to be specific."

When she got to Daniel and me, I spoke up. "I have two prosthetic legs, and I'm a snowboarder," I said. "I want to help youth and young adults with disabilities learn how to snowboard and skateboard."

Her eyes lit up. "That's the most concrete idea I've heard tonight," she said. "I think you can make it work."

The teacher loved our idea so much that she agreed to work with us after the class; Daniel's mom also helped us. They guided us through every step we needed to take to create a 501(c)(3) organization, like choosing a name, putting a board of directors in place, coming up with bylaws and articles of incorporation, and preparing state and federal filings. Picking the right name was very important to me: My story had gotten some local press in the Sunday paper, and many organizations with words like *disabled* and *handicapped* in their names had reached out to me for partnership. I was always turned off by those terms. I wanted to focus on capabilities, not disabilities, and I wanted our organization to draw people with that mind-set.

After days of brainstorming, Daniel and I finally settled on our name: Adaptive Action Sports (AAS). I loved the word *adaptive* because it suggests an attitude of "You'll find a way," whatever it takes. And the "action sports" part of our name would include not just snowboarding and skateboarding—but also sports such as rock climbing, rally car racing, and motocross, among others.

My friend Beth, who was in and out of acting roles in Hollywood, was still dating the actor Jason Lee around the time we came up with our idea, and in addition to being an actor, Jason is also a professional skateboarder. When Beth mentioned our nonprofit idea to Jason, he loved it; he even agreed to throw the first fund-raisers: an art show in Los Angeles and another in New York. Between those two events, he raised $30,000, enough for us to launch the organization. By summer 2005, Adaptive Action Sports was officially set up and ready to go.

The first project sponsored by AAS: a rock-climbing camp. A friend of ours had been trying to organize the camp in Tahoe, because he knew some athletes there who wanted to learn, so we gave him a grant to fund it. Then as our work in the organization got even more fully under way that first year, we gave funds to a group of skateboarders with prosthetics who wanted to enter a competition. From the start, we'd decided we wanted AAS to be national; we wanted our nonprofit to flourish well enough that Daniel and I could work on it full-time as co–executive directors. Until we could get to that point, however, we kept our day jobs, and we worked on AAS together in the evenings and on weekends.

One of our first big goals with AAS: Daniel and I wanted to get adaptive snowboarding into the X Games, an annual ESPN action sport competition that, at the time, was like the Olympics for action sports. At nineteen when I was stuck in my hospital bed, flipping through the TV channels, I remember watching the Summer X Games—and if I could have seen just one athlete with a prosthetic leg, it would've been such an encouragement to me. Our other grand vision was to get adaptive snowboarding into the Paralympic Games. Snowboarding was already an Olympic sport, so why shouldn't it also be a Paralympic one?

So in the months and years that followed, we pursued a mission. We began regularly organizing and hosting snowboard camps and clinics, a place where our athletes could come and progress in their sport, as well as create a sense of community. At our camps, snowboarders could take lessons and train to compete at an elite level. We also collaborated with other organizations, like CAF, to bring athletes to our camps. In addition, we organized adaptive snowboard competitions with USASA (United States of America Snowboard Association) so that our athletes would have a place to compete.

I loved working on our organization. Before we'd moved to San Diego, we'd thought we'd get away to the Big Bear resort in Southern California's San Bernardino Mountains and snowboard just for fun, but once the business took off, we really didn't get away at all. I'd sometimes stay up all night working, looking for lodging, finding sponsors, organizing the clinics. Thanks to my parents, I'm very entrepreneurial, so I enjoyed taking the reins and creating something meaningful for other people. Daniel and I made a great team. He's more of the visionary, and I'm more of the hands-on doer. We didn't see our organization as just another nonprofit; we saw it as a powerful movement—a way for us to bring athletes together to do the seemingly impossible, to blur the line between ability and disability. We still view it that way.

I'VE LEARNED THAT when you have any kind of desire, it's important to talk about it and put it out there into the universe. I've always wanted to perform. So everywhere I went, I'd say to people, "I'd love to move to L.A. and try acting." I'd said that to my prosthetist, Kevin, many times, and one day in 2005, Kevin got an email from an indie film producer who was looking for an actor: a female in her twenties with reddish brown hair, an artsy vintage style, and one prosthetic leg. Because Kevin knew of my desire to act, he connected me with the producer.

I called him immediately. "This is Amy Purdy," I said. "My

prosthetist told me you've been searching for an actress with one prosthetic leg. I have two, but I'd still really love to audition for the role." Never mind that I had no acting experience—none.

"Okay," he said. "I'll send you the script." He did, and I immediately called Beth to get some pointers on the best way to prepare. The character I was to play was Alma, a soft-spoken girl who didn't quite feel confident in what she was doing, which was the perfect first role for me, because neither did I!

About a week after the producer's call, I drove to Los Angeles to audition. When I walked into the lobby, I saw all these other young women who were clearly trying out for the role. Everyone in that waiting room had reddish brown hair, although I was the only one with prosthetic legs. If the director couldn't find an actor with a prosthetic, I'd been told, he'd have to hire someone else and then pretend she was missing a leg.

I did my audition, and though I was nervous, I thought it went well. Afterward, I had a chance to talk with the director, Eli Steele, briefly. "I know you're looking for someone with one prosthetic leg," I said, "and I've got two. But there's no good reason why this character should have just one prosthetic." He nodded and smiled but didn't say much. I must've gotten through to him, because soon after, I received the exciting news: I had gotten the role. The film, which is about a young deaf man (actor Ross Thomas) who finds himself in a love triangle between a dream girl (Nora Kirkpatrick) and a real girl (me), is called *What's Bugging Seth*.

I was beyond elated. I took a leave from my spa job, and Daniel agreed to continue work on AAS while I was away. For the next two months, I drove between San Diego and Los Angeles for rehearsals. While in town, I hung out with Beth and Jason. Once the rehearsals were complete, I then relocated to Carmel in Northern California for the shooting. I lived in this charming, cottage-like house with a makeup artist and one of the other actors, Nora; she and Ross were both serious performers who'd previously had roles. As the newbie of the group, I was definitely out of my comfort zone, but that's often where you need to be in order to stretch yourself. I'm notorious for putting myself in uncomfortable situations. I have a "jump now, look later" mentality. I'd soon find out if I'd leapt too quickly.

I was so green that I thought I had to memorize the entire script, which is what I'd done the whole night before the first day of filming. Once my hair and makeup was done that afternoon, I went to the set. I was to be in the first scene, which was in a café at dusk on a main street in nearby Monterey. The crew had shut down the entire street just for our shoot. Along the street, there were film trailers, lights, the works. My hands actually quivered as I awaited the director's instructions. A few minutes later, I heard that frightening word: "Action!" I suddenly wanted to die.

Trying to hide my nervousness, I walked confidently to my place on the set and began delivering my opening line, I was so nervous that I could hear my heartbeat in my voice. I didn't get very far before the director yelled out, "Cut!" and pulled me aside.

"Okay, so you're a little nervous," he said. "Just take a couple of deep breaths and let's do this again." All I could think about was how many other actors, some of whom actually would've known what they were doing, I beat out for this role. Oh, the pressure.

My second attempt wasn't much better, but I did at least manage to get through the scene without any major fumbles. My nervousness was so palpable that I couldn't really focus on making my character as warm and comfortable as she was supposed to appear in that scene. Oh well. It had been sink or swim, and though I swam, it was more like a dog paddle.

Later that evening, I called Daniel. "I do not want to be here," I told him through tears. "I have such a belief in myself that I can accomplish things, but then when I get into them, I realize I don't know what the hell I am doing!" Daniel tried to calm me down. "I believe in you, babe," he said. "You've got this. I know you can do it, and so do they. The director wouldn't have hired you if he didn't think you could pull it off."

Daniel's pep talk was enough to get me back onto the set for day two, which went far more smoothly. For one thing, I wasn't trying to hold an entire script in my head: I gave up all that memorizing and just focused on what I needed to know for the current day. That second afternoon, as I was standing on the set with Ross, I asked him, "Don't you ever get nervous?" I will forever remember what he told me: "Yeah, I do get nervous—but nerves are energy," he said. "You can either use that energy negatively or positively. If I'm in an emotional scene and I need to cry, I use the nervous energy as emotion. If I need to laugh, I use the energy as happiness. You just have to channel your energy in the right direction." Words of wisdom I learned to use, both on the stage and in my life.

Over the next several weeks, I went from feeling completely overwhelmed to feeling somewhat confident in my skills. Once I relaxed, I actually enjoyed developing the character. I did have a couple of things in common with Alma, but one big difference had to do with our legs: Alma always wanted to hide her prosthetics; in my own life, I'd gotten to the point where I was actually proud to show my metal parts. I was in the second-highest number of scenes (after Ross), and every day, I got up and put on my legs with pride. I'd turned the corner: My legs weren't just something I attached to my body. They were extensions of me.

We filmed for six weeks. By the end, I might not have been in the same league with the other actors in that film, but I'd definitely proven to myself that I could get better, and I'd crossed off yet another goal on my life's to-do list. When the film premiered in Newport Beach, California, in April 2005, it did very well on the worldwide indie circuit. It won first place at the Fargo Film Festival. It also won awards from the San Fernando Valley Film Festival, the Santa Cruz Film Festival, and several others. My family and Daniel joined me at the premiere, and it is the strangest thing to see yourself up on the big screen. There are moments when I wanted to cringe, scenes in which I thought, *Well, I hope it looks better than it felt;* yet there were other moments when I recognized just how much I'd grown in six short, voice-quaking, hand-tremoring weeks.

"I WANT TO move to L.A." That's the announcement I made to Daniel one spring evening in 2006. After landing that lead role the year before, I wanted to keep my acting momentum going. I longed to play all kinds of characters, and I also dreamed of starring in a mainstream film. Plus, I'd really connected with Beth, Jason, and many of their actor and artist friends, and I'd often drive up to Los Angeles on the weekends. It was exactly the kind of community I craved. Daniel and I had already been casually discussing a possible move. But about a year after returning from Carmel, I decided it really was time for me to head for Hollywood.

Daniel was open to the idea. His only request was that we live near a beach; not only did he love the laid-back culture and party scene, but he also wanted to continue working as a surf instructor. So once we settled on that compromise, all there was left to do was pack up, give our notices at work, and drive north two hours. In fall 2006, we moved into a small apartment tucked away in a neighborhood near Venice Beach. We'd been lucky to find a relatively inexpensive beach apartment in San Diego, but this one in Venice wasn't so cheap—$1,500 a month for a one-bedroom with an oven the size of an Easy Bake. That was a lot for us.

I looked for work right away. I landed two part-time spa jobs. One was at a new place called the Lounge Spa, and the other was at the Beverly Hilton. I also signed up for an evening acting class. My goal was to challenge myself to really improve my skills. So between working during the day, taking the course, and spending time on our organization, there was very little time for anything else but sleep, and on some days, there wasn't much time even for that.

We only stayed in Los Angeles for a year and a half, and stress from work and financial pressures made this one of the toughest chapters in our relationship. Toward the end of our time there, the economy began to slide toward full recession; people just weren't spending as much on the extras, like massages and facials, as they were once willing to spend, so my income dipped. I'd sometimes be on call for a full day and get only a fifteen-dollar brow wax; and rather than spending on a pricey massage at a fancy hotel like the Beverly Hilton, many clients went looking for inexpensive alternatives in their own neighborhoods. I loved the quality of our service at the Beverly, but we just didn't have enough of a clientele to keep me busy during that period.

Daniel wanted to re-enroll in school and finish a few classes, and because most of his credits wouldn't transfer elsewhere, he wanted to return to Gunnison, Colorado, just outside Crested Butte. We'd only need to stay for a year because Daniel was close to being done—and while he hadn't regretted taking a break, he did want to finally complete the degree. So in late 2007, we moved back to the Colorado mountains. Frankly, as disappointed as I was that I hadn't really developed my acting, I was ready to go. I was so tired of living paycheck to paycheck. And I wanted to get Roxy back. Not only was I longing to reunite with her, but I knew how much she'd love the mountains.

Once we found a place in Colorado, some of our financial pressures were eased right away. We paid eight hundred dollars a month for a gorgeous two-story, three-bedroom house with marble countertops throughout. The house was near a river and a horse pasture; the beautiful Crested Butte Mountain Resort was just forty minutes away. It smelled amazing outside. I loved the scent of the fresh grass. We rode our bikes, and Roxy was right there running alongside us, her floppy ears flapping in the wind. The whole environment was healthy; it was great to be back where we could really breathe, especially after all that smog and traffic congestion. As Daniel went to school, I worked on the organization full-time. That's the plan we'd agreed on for our year there. By the time we returned to Colorado, Daniel had already laid a solid groundwork for us to get snowboarding into the X Games. We both became determined to see that happen—one way or another.

CHAPTER 13

Transition

"All great changes are preceded by chaos."

—DEEPAK CHOPRA

Our year in Colorado passed quickly. As I forged ahead with work on the nonprofit, Daniel completed some of his coursework; being back in the program clarified for him that resort management just wasn't his true passion. Instead, he wanted to devote his full energy to building our organization. So in 2008, once he finished the last course he wanted to take, we decided to move again. We relocated to the one place I'd been dreaming of for much of my life—Lake Tahoe.

Tahoe was everything I'd imagined, and even more gorgeous than that. Pine trees that gave off an amazing scent surrounded our house. The lake itself was stunning: crystalline waters that became even more beautiful when the light hit the surface. On many summer evenings, Daniel and I hiked out to the lake with a bottle of wine and some cheese and crackers and enjoyed our own little picnic. I'd sit there, gazing out over the water, wondering whether my mom and dad had once sat in exactly the same spot, enjoying the same brilliant yellow-orange sunset. Other times, we'd light a fire, have a barbecue, and just sit outside and soak in the beauty of the nature around us.

I took an on-call massage job at a small spa, and we continued our push to get adaptive snowboarding into the X Games. While we were still in Los Angeles, Daniel had approached the higher-ups at ESPN. He presented our idea, but they chose to pass. "What other sports are part of your organization?" one of the executives asked. Daniel gave them the list, and they seemed to latch on to adaptive motocross. We were disappointed that they hadn't wanted to move forward with snowboarding, but we quickly shifted gears and focused on getting motocross into the Summer X Games. Our persistence paid off. By spring 2008, the executives had decided to add adaptive motocross to that year's list of summer sports; we also got an adaptive skateboard exhibition into the X Games. Once athletes heard about the motocross competition, they flocked to the X Games from all over the world, just for the chance to compete. Daniel and I were elated. After you put so much energy into a project, it's very fulfilling to see it work out. Few experiences compare.

Around this time, a few more media opportunities cropped up. *Women's Health* magazine did a feature story about my life; soon after, I was invited to speak at a women's conference. It was a corporate event, and when they asked me for my fee, I had no idea what to charge. So I threw out a random number: $8,000. They agreed to pay me that fee and I began preparing the speech. I nearly drove myself insane, trying to come up with just the right stories to tell and the best way to arrange the talk. Where should I begin? I was in panic mode. I stopped eating. I'd start a draft and then ball it up and throw it in the trash. I could barely even sleep. I nearly made myself sick with worry. How do you boil nearly thirty years of life into thirty or forty minutes? I'm shocked Daniel didn't walk out on me, because for a short time, I lost my mind.

I felt so much pressure trying to prepare a speech worthy of $8,000 that I actually backed out—the first and last time I've ever walked away from a big commitment. Yes, for years, I'd wanted to speak, but wanting to speak versus actually *delivering* a great motivational speech are two different things. I wish I'd said I would do it for free, because $8,000 dollars made the stakes too high for a first speech. So I did begin speaking voluntarily, just to get some experience. I also took a speaking course, and though what I learned there wasn't exactly groundbreaking, it at least got me thinking about the best way to tell my story. Each time I did, it became slightly more comfortable—a little easier to open up without quivering.

I'M INTO VISION boards. So in summer 2009, I put up a small corkboard on the bedroom wall of our home in Tahoe. The board was one of the first things I saw when I got up every morning. I filled it with words and images related to experiences I wanted to have. Playing the piano. Traveling. Owning a home. I even had a photo of Chris Farley from *SNL* as a motivational speaker. At some point, I ripped out an ad for Element Eden, a skateboard and apparel company that encourages social activism. I respected the work of

Element Skateboards (the company that owns Element Eden) and had once met the marketing director at one of our events.

Well, one morning a few months after I put that ad on my board, I got a call. "This is Jardine Hammond from Element Eden. I don't know if you remember me, but we're doing a photo shoot in Newport Beach tomorrow, and we think you'd be perfect for it. I don't even know if you're in California or close by, but I'd love for you to come." The photo shoot, called "Power to the Planet," was part of an ad campaign featuring those overcoming limits and just doing interesting things with their lives; it included professional skateboarders, artists, and musicians. Not only did I have the time and interest, but I was visiting Los Angeles, completing a free-lance job, when I got Jardine's call. "Yes, I'd love to do it," I told her. It felt meant to be.

I got there, and wouldn't you know it, a girl who'd been in the ad on my vision board was being photographed! That day, I met Johnny Schillereff, the founder of Element. Johnny, a former pro-fessional skateboarder, is a huge part of why the sport has become what it is. He invited me and a few of the skateboarders there to join him for a dinner that evening, and he also asked me to sit at his table. "The minute I saw you today," he told me, "I just thought you were the coolest thing! I told my wife all about you." That night, we ended up having an amazing conversation, and the following day, I visited the Element offices. He asked me to be an Advocate—one of several skateboarders, artists, and humanitarians who are making a difference in the world and who represent Element. I agreed and we promised to stay in touch.

A month later, Johnny called me. "A speaking opportunity has come up," he said. "I've been invited to share my story with twelve hundred students at Newport Beach High School. It would be great if you could join me and speak as well for a few minutes."

"Absolutely," I said right away. Not only would it give me another round of practice at speaking, but ten minutes of talking with students is far less intimidating than an hour of speaking to corporate business people. I was actually excited about this.

So Johnny first gave his talk, and then he looked over at me with an expression that said, "Okay, are you ready to share now?" I was. I'd had forty minutes to sit there and get comfortable in the gymnasium as Johnny spoke. So I walked up to the podium. My hands shook a little. But then I began exactly the way I'd practiced. "I'm Amy Purdy, and here is my story." Over the next fifteen minutes, you could hear a pin drop as I talked. Afterward, dozens of students flowed up to the front to talk with me one-on-one. Some wanted to hug me or take a photo with me; others were near tears as they shared some of the difficulties they'd had to overcome. In the following months, I did another speech with Johnny, and then I was invited to be the keynote speaker at a youth conference for high schoolers all over the Newport Beach area. Each time I took the stage, I became more confident, and that confidence increased the resonance of my story.

In September 2009, I overheard Johnny talking to the marketing director about a trip they were planning "We're teaming up with Toms shoes to take hundreds of skateboards and thousands of shoes to children in South Africa," he explained. He wasn't going himself, but he was sending a few people from his company for the two-week trip. This sounded like the opportunity of a lifetime. So the next day, I sent Johnny an email. "If you're looking for another person to go to Africa," I wrote, "I'd love to go." Not even ten minutes later, he responded with "You're in." Ha! Sometimes all you have to do is ask.

From there, the plan took shape. That October, a team of us would fly out of Los Angeles together for a project called "the South African Shoe Drop." I was over the moon! I'd been needing to have some work done on my legs, so before leaving for such a faraway land, I knew I'd have to first stop in Vegas and see Kevin. This was to be my very first big international trip, and I wanted to be sure I was in tip-top shape.

WHILE THE BIG South Africa adventure awaited, I became increasingly frustrated with our financial situation. We were living right on the edge. Just to make the rent, I took on some freelance work, but even with that income, I was still having to borrow money at times from my parents. They were fine with that—but I wasn't. I wanted to make my own money. Pay my own bills. Work toward my own plan for financial security.

The years of monetary struggle weighed heavily on my relationship with Daniel. Things became even more tense between us than they'd been in Venice. We had big arguments frequently. I knew that at some point in my life, I could possibly need another kidney transplant—there's always that risk, even years down the line—and where would I get the money? The more I worried, the more I brought up our financial future. I wanted him to have the same sense of urgency that I did to set up our lives so that we'd have some financial stability. I started to realize that I'd been selfishly relying on him to provide that security, but I needed to provide it for myself.

Our business partnership also became strained. I wanted

everything to run smoothly, for the details of our nonprofit work to be completely in our control, so I found myself micromanaging, with questions like "Did you get around to sending out that email today?" That wasn't good for either one of us, and of course, it was irritating to Daniel. Our communication suffered.

When I reflected on all the years we'd already spent together, I could see that we were caught in some unhealthy patterns. I could also see that we were growing in different directions. And though I still loved him with all my heart and cherished him as my best friend, I felt strongly that we needed some time apart. We'd still be somewhat connected, of course, because we had the organization to oversee. But even as we kept AAS going, I knew we needed some space from one another. "We both need to step away, make some changes in our lives, and stand on our own two feet," I said in a tearful conversation. "And then if we decide to come back together, we'll each come back whole." Daniel didn't see it that way at all—he wanted us to work out our differences while staying in the relationship. But I'd made up my mind that I needed the freedom to go my own way for a while. So right after I'd been invited on the South Africa trip, Daniel and I separated. He stayed in Tahoe. And rather than simply stopping over in Vegas to have my legs worked on, I made plans to move back there indefinitely.

CHAPTER 14

Horizons

"I haven't been everywhere, but it's on my list."

—SUSAN SONTAG

I was running late. My friend in Vegas, the former high school classmate I'd moved in with once I returned to my hometown, raced me to the airport for my flight to Los Angeles International Airport; that's where I'd meet the rest of the team for our trip to South Africa. When I got up to the counter in the Vegas airport, I handed my driver's license to the agent. "I'm on the next flight to Los Angeles," I announced breathlessly.

"Miss Purdy?" she said, eyeing my license as she pecked at her keyboard. "I'm sorry, but you're not going to be able to get onto this flight."

"What do you mean I can't get on the flight?"

"You have to be here a full hour before the flight in order to keep your seat," she said. "If you're not checked in on time, your seat goes to the next person on the standby list. I'll have to rebook you on the next flight."

I glanced down at my watch. I'd missed the deadline by two minutes—*two*. "Can you please just get me in?"

"Sorry, ma'am, but that's airline policy."

"Listen, I'm going to South Africa later today, and we're doing a huge shoe donation to some poor children there," I said loudly, hoping that someone in the long line behind me would overhear my story and take pity on me. No one blinked. "If I miss this flight, then I'll also miss my flight from L.A. to South Africa. Is there anything at all you can do to help me get to South Africa?"

"Nope," she said, hardly looking up from her keyboard. She handed me back my license and the new ticket. "I've already put you on the next flight. It'll leave here three hours from now." I lost it. After staring up at an overhead flight monitor for a second, I made my way directly to the gate of my original flight, the one I was apparently missing.

"Excuse me, ladies and gentlemen," I said to forty or so people waiting in the lounge area. "My name is Amy Purdy, and as you can see I have two prosthetic legs." I had to pull out my trump card. People stared down at my metal parts. "I'm on my way to South Africa to give away shoes to impoverished children in the villages, and I don't even have feet myself. If I don't make this flight to Los Angeles, I cannot help these kids. Will anyone here be kind enough to go on the next flight and let me take your seat?" Total silence. I could read on their faces what they were thinking: *This girl is crazy.* I then began pleading my case with the agent at the gate counter. She didn't budge.

A few minutes later, all the passengers in that waiting area filed onto the plane and the door slammed shut. My chance was over. Right then, there was a shift switch, and a new agent, a tall black man, took his place behind the ticket counter. He noticed me bawling in my seat nearby.

"What's going on?" he asked. I stood up and walked over to the counter. "I missed this last flight to L.A.," I said, wiping away a tear, "and now I can't get to South Africa." I told him the whole story of the volunteer shoe drop. He looked directly at me. "Well," he said in a booming voice, "nobody is going to be denied a trip to my home country because of a missed flight!" Then without another word, he dashed over to the plane door, radioed the flight attendant to open it for him, and marched down the corridor. When he returned, he had a passenger with him, someone who'd volunteered to take a later flight. "Go take your seat," he said, wearing a huge smile. I jumped right up, profusely thanked the man who'd given me his spot, and raced down the walkway to my flight. I couldn't believe I'd made it on! Running into this amazing agent who just so happened to be from the very country I was visiting is just one more piece of evidence that everything happens for a reason.

I made it to Los Angeles, met up with the others, and boarded the flight on to South Africa. As excited as I'd been in the days leading up to the trip, I suddenly got scared. My mind raced with questions: *What will it be like to take this trip without Daniel— the one person I've walked through most of my adult life with? How will it feel to travel with people I barely even know? And what if I get sick?* I'd soon find out.

When Johnny offered me the trip to South Africa, I'd envisioned villagers who lived in grass-covered mud huts. When we arrived in Durban, I quickly discovered how wrong I was. As we drove from the airport into the city, I was surprised by how developed the place seemed. It looked like the kind of city you'd find in many parts of the United States. We drove through neighborhoods filled with grassy yards and children playing soccer in pretty parks. The grocery stores looked clean and modern. The people were neatly dressed. We checked into a cozy, cottagelike Victorian bed-and-breakfast run by a friendly local couple. "You have to be careful about the baboons," the wife warned us with a smile. "They're quite naughty! Keep your windows closed."

After a short stay in Durban, we finally made our way out to the villages to begin the shoe drop. The villages looked nothing like the mud huts I'd pictured. They were well manicured, and many of the villagers were out farming the picturesque gardens and land when we arrived. Yet appearances aside, the reality of village life can be hard to fathom. "In this area," said our tour guide as we rode in on a bus from Durban, "one in four babies die from malnutrition." And many of the kids succumb to HIV either because they don't know they have it, they're fearful of seeking medical care given the stigma the disease has in their communities, or they can't get medical care.

And the scores of adorable village children were just too sweet. You should have seen all their cute little faces! When we pulled out the shoes and put them on their feet, some of them wept. Others danced and sang. Many shyly whispered, "Thank you." The condition of their old shoes saddened me. Many children wore shoes that were three sizes too small. I wanted to run back home to America, gather up my dozens of pairs of shoes, and return to add them to the twenty thousand pairs we gave out. Ironically, I had no feet, but did have more shoes than I could ever wear. They had both their feet, yet never enough shoes to go around.

Before I left, my mom kept saying, "You're going to have the time of your life." And I did. I came home with so many unforgettable memories. Like observing the simple pleasure the children experienced as they played with the empty shoe boxes we left behind. Meeting a group of village women who fed us a delicious meal of goat, plus beets and sweet potatoes straight from their own garden. Spotting a stunning cheetah walking along the horizon one evening—and later seeing another that came within five feet of me in our jeep ride through a nature reserve. Witnessing the herd of massive bull elephants who swarmed near our private retreat on our final day, wrapping their trunks around the aloe trees to strip away the leaves, then sucking water from the Jacuzzi and blowing it out all over the place as if to bid us farewell for our travels home.

"The darkest thing about Africa has always been our ignorance of it," George Kimball, a geographer, once said. In one magnificent journey—not vicariously through the pages of my *National Geographic,* but up close and through my own eyes—I discovered so much light on a continent that's often feared and seldom understood. Not only did I return home with a desire to always be part of giving back; I also realized that I'd been given an incredible gift—a recognition. As different and as far away as the people of South Africa may seem to some, they are really not at all different from you and me. We may be separated by oceans and continents, but we all still have hopes, passions, goals, and dreams. Mothers want the best for their children. Children want to be nurtured. And people all over the planet—from South Africa to the

United States and beyond—simply want to be affirmed. Validated. Loved.

THE HIGH I felt after my big adventure lasted for about three weeks. As life settled back into a normal rhythm, I felt my mood slide downhill. I was back in Vegas. Again. And this time, I didn't have parents or a sister nearby. They'd all moved to Boise, Idaho, because they thought it would be a great environment for my sister's children to grow up in; they could play in the foothills and rivers and really know their neighbors. My aunts and cousins were all still around, and I felt close to them. But when I'd call up old friends around Vegas and ask them to hang out, they were busy with their families. Their lives had moved on.

I kept myself occupied with work. I added a new item to my vision board—a dollar figure of $35,000. That's the amount of additional money I wanted to earn by the end of that year, whether it was through my speaking engagements, my work with Element, or other kinds of work I could line up for myself. In one of my favorite books, *Your Thoughts Can Change Your Life,* I read a line I loved: "To bring something into your life, imagine that it is already there." That is exactly what I began to do.

One evening in February 2011, I opened my email and scrolled through the messages. I stopped when I saw the subject line "Speaking Event." The email was from Linda, a woman who'd organized that Newport Beach event I spoke at in 2009. I opened the email, and without reading the main message, I went straight to downloading the attachment. It was a beautifully put-together PowerPoint presentation. On the first slide, I saw the phrase "TED."

"We invite you to give . . . to give the speech of your lifetime . . . in 18 minutes or less . . . on May 18, 2011." I just about fainted.

I loved TED. Daniel had introduced me to it a few years before, and I'd watched several inspiring talks. So I was plenty aware that giving a TED speech could launch an entire career. I'd even fantasized about one day giving my own talk, maybe when I was like forty-five and experienced enough. The TED team had forwarded the invite to Linda, and she was passing it along to me. There was a phone number and contact name listed for TEDxOrangeCoast. I called right away.

"Hello, yes, this is Amy Purdy," I said, trying to enunciate each word and use my best speechmaking voice. "I just received an invitation to do a speech through your organization. I'd really love to participate."

"Yes, hello, Amy!" said the woman. "That's wonderful. We've been excited about the possibility of your speech."

"How did you even hear about me?" I asked.

"Well, a flyer from the Newport Beach event ended up on my desk, and the little I read about you fascinated me," she explained. She'd reached out to the event's organizer, Linda, so she could get in touch with me. I couldn't believe it.

Once I realized that this was actually *real*, I started freaking out. And then I did my best to rechannel that freak-out energy into a clear focus. "I could either use this to create a massive platform," I later told Daniel, "or I could just get through it. It's my choice, really." The TEDx organizer had told me that the theme of the event was breaking down borders. My mind began racing with ideas of all the different parts of my story I could share.

The stakes were high for this speech, so I put some serious

pressure on myself. I thought, *If this were the only speech I were to ever give, what would I want to say?* I wrote down a whole jumble of stories that I didn't know how to string together into one coherent speech. This went on for weeks, and I still couldn't get it organized. And with every day that ticked by, bringing me closer to May 18, I became more of a lunatic.

Two weeks before the event, TEDx set me up with one of their speaking coaches, a woman named Barbara. We set up a Skype call so I could read my speech for her. "I love it," she told me afterward. "You've clearly done some great work already. But I want to go deeper." Deeper? I argued with her about that at first, but then I realized she was right. I was just skimming over the hardest topics, like losing my legs and the transplant, without really sharing my full *feelings* about those experiences. "I want you to bring the same feeling to it that you felt when you went through it." So I created a second draft, which she liked. But over the next few days, that draft got chopped. And chopped. And chopped again. By two days before the speech, they'd taken me from the promised eighteen minutes down to eight minutes. Several other people were giving speeches that day to a live audience of over 1,500 people, and the time had to be reallocated. I was a mess, but I made the cuts. "Now you need to memorize it," she told me.

The day of the speech arrived. I drove to the gorgeous, auditorium-style theater in Orange County; it looked like an opera house. I was intimidated right away: When I scanned the agenda, I could see that the other speakers were experts in their fields, some of the most brilliant minds in the country. Who was I to be there? "Let's do a short rehearsal," Barbara suggested. So I performed the entire speech—and I completely messed it up. My mind got scrambled and I couldn't remember most of what I'd memorized.

"I dont know if I can do this!" I said with tears welling up. I was also crying because of all the pent-up stress that had been building over the last three months. I started pacing and trying to recite. "What if I get emotional?"

Barbara did her best to calm me down. "Right now," she said, "you just have to put your faith in God that if you get emotional, it will be at the right time."

I stood backstage, listening for my name to be called. As I waited, I thought, *Okay, Barbara is right: I've just got to turn this over and do what I can. I've done the work. Now I've just gotta go out there and enjoy it.* I felt dizzy, and my heart fluttered in my chest. At last, I heard my name: "Ladies and gentlemen, please welcome Amy Purdy," and then applause. I walked out, cleared my throat, and began. "If your life were a book, and you were the author," I said, "how would you want your story to go?" I paused and drew in a quick breath, as if to fuel myself for the coming words. "That's the question that changed my life forever." The room, which was already fairly quiet, fell utterly silent. Over the next eight minutes as I spoke, my hands shook, my voice cracked a bit, and yet my story flowed from the most raw and honest place I'd ever talked from.

"Maybe instead of looking at our challenges and limitations as something negative or bad," I said in closing, "we can begin to look at them as blessings—magnificent gifts that can be used to ignite our imaginations and help us go farther than we ever knew we could go. It's not about breaking down borders, it's about push-ing off of them, and seeing what amazing places they might bring us." When I looked out at the audience, every single person in the front was crying. Even a few old guys were taking off their bifocals to wipe away tears. I knew I had done it. I'd delivered a speech made perfect by its imperfections. That's what made it the speech of my lifetime.

Less than a month after that speech, my sweet Roxy—my angel dog—passed away; two months before, a vet had diagnosed her with bladder cancer. She'd stayed alive just long enough to walk with me through TED. She spent long afternoons at my side, sniffing around, chasing prairie dogs, and bringing me the same joy she always had. I believe that dogs, like humans, sometimes stay alive just to care for us through a tough season. When Roxy finally transitioned on June 10, 2011, she did so at a critical juncture in my story. I couldn't have known it then—but my life and career were about to take off.

DANIEL AND I reunited. Our separation wasn't years long, but it didn't need to be. We'd learned what we needed to learn. I'd proven to myself that I could move toward my own financial dreams without placing the expectation on Daniel to do it for me. For his part, Daniel had squeezed a decade of growth into a single year. He'd become very focused on the nonprofit. It was clear that not only could he be the powerful visionary he has always been; he'd also developed enough discipline to oversee the details. While we'd been growing in our own directions, we'd also grown to love each other even more. Sometimes you have to completely let go of someone in order to remember what you most cherished about that person on day one. We wanted to be together, but Daniel didn't want to move to Boise, and I wasn't going back to Tahoe. So we made plans to come together in Crested Butte in the winter of 2011.

The number on the vision board turned out to be prophetic. By the end of 2010, I'd earned almost exactly $35,000 more, nearly down to the penny. I thought, *Why didn't I put $200,000 on my vision board!?* You'd better believe I at least increased it to $100,000 after that! I'd shown myself that I could actually make a living at what I loved. I thought the requests would come rolling in after the TEDxOrangeCoast speech, but initially, there wasn't much buzz. Once my speech was posted online, it received less than a thousand page-views.

But in fall 2011, I got this email from the national TED team: "Out of hundreds of speeches considered," read the note, "your speech has been chosen to go live on the home page of TED.com tomorrow." When I clicked on the next morning, I already had more than forty thousand page-views! Since then, my speech has been translated into multiple languages and has been viewed and shared millions of times. And to think I almost walked away from it because it was so hard to prepare. After the home page posting, the speaking requests poured in from all over the world, and I began climbing my way up to become a highly-requested motivational speaker. My fees grew larger as I did my research and got courageous enough to ask for a competitive rate. That meant I had more money to build a safety net for myself, as well as the cash to put into our organization.

Daniel and I began hosting even more snowboarding camps and competitions, which was the best way to grow the sport. In 2011, I myself competed in snowboarding in France and came home with two golds; then I competed in New Zealand and earned one gold. At the time, companies wouldn't yet sponsor us because we weren't recognized as an official sport yet, which is why our athletes usually traveled to these events on their own dime, as I did for the New Zealand competition. Hosting and participating in competitions was part of our strategy for proving that adaptive snowboarding *should* be an official sport.

One huge victory came as a result of that strategy. In 2011, we were at last successful in getting Adaptive Snowboard Cross into the Winter X Games. Daniel and I were ecstatic. We tried to use that triumph to show the Paralympic Committee what we were capable of. As the numbers of athletes we trained and the frequency of our world competitions increased, we also partnered with a few international snowboarding organizations to make one giant push to have our sport included in the 2014 Paralympic Games in Sochi. We became very hopeful about our prospects when a member of the Russian Paralympic Committee came to our world cup in New Zealand. In fact, when I stood on top of the podium to receive my award, it was that very committee member who hung the gold medallion around my neck. I could already envision myself in Sochi. We all could.

CHAPTER 15

The Race

"Life is either a daring adventure or nothing at all."
—HELEN KELLER

Exactly one hour after our 2011 World Cup closing ceremony in New Zealand, we got a press release. The 2014 Paralympic Committee would not include our sport in the Sochi Paralympics.

"Are you serious?" I said, throwing my hands in the air after reading the email. Daniel was just as dumbfounded.

"Wow, I was almost one hundred percent sure we had that in the bag," he said. From the day we began AAS, this had been our one big goal for the only sport that has ever made me feel fully alive. And now our dream wasn't going to happen. We were crushed.

We returned home to Crested Butte, and you've never seen such long faces. "What do I even *do* at this point?" I said to Daniel. We'd been so excited about the possibility of Sochi that I'd already mapped out a plan: I would train for the three years leading up to the 2014 Paralympics. But when life doesn't go as planned—and don't I know all about that—I've learned you just have to regroup. I did that by more fully immersing myself in the world of speaking. If I couldn't get our sport into the Sochi games, I could at least make a career of sharing my stories and the lessons I've learned. We still ran our snowboard camps and clinics, but some of the excitement surrounding our work dissipated after such a major letdown.

Our disappointment didn't have time to settle in, because soon after, we got some great news. Daniel and I were chosen to be on Season 21 of *The Amazing Race,* that reality show in which teams of two try to outrace each other to different parts of the globe. The producers at the CBS show had previously connected with us through a friend of mine, a Paralympic athlete; when my friend and his girlfriend realized they couldn't do the race, they suggested me and Daniel as their replacements. In the end, we weren't chosen for that round, but for this second time around, we were in.

Daniel and I set out to win. We were resourceful and well-traveled. We'd spent enough years together, working out our differences, that we could set aside the silly arguments that often come up between couples on the show. We would stay focused on the journey in front of us. We would run our race like we ran our lives and business: Courageously. Intensely. Efficiently. And while having as much fun as possible. In addition, I'd already decided my legs weren't going to stop me. Daniel and I were planning on giving the other competitors a run for their money.

At the starting line on a Pasadena, California, bridge with the ten other teams (among them, a set of Sri Lankan twins, engaged lumberjacks, two Chippendales, and a monster trucker couple), the stakes were immediately raised. Phil Keoghan, the show's host, announced, "For the first time in *Amazing Race* history, you have the chance to double your money! Here's how it works: If your team wins the first and last leg of the race, you will win . . . two million dollars!" The others cheered, and Daniel and I exchanged a look that said, "Oh, yeah: We're winning this thing."

But we didn't. Not by a long shot. We got off to a good start (we rappelled from a bridge and were one of the first teams down) and received our initial clue, which sent us all the way to Shanghai. From there, the short version of our race is that Daniel got killed in a table tennis match against a ten-year-old Chinese national champion; we both scarfed down what we thought were white noodles in an emptied papaya bowl (but which were actually frog fallopian tubes, a traditional Chinese dessert); we made a stop at the Bund (a gorgeous Shanghai waterfront area), where we had to find a woman with an abacus, which is an ancient counting instrument; and after starting out in second place in Indonesia, we lost four hours because our taxi driver couldn't find a "Wijaya Motors" (there are several of them, and our cabbie must have driven us to every single one except for the *right* one). We got eliminated at only the second pit stop, the one in Surabaya, Indonesia.

The loss was disappointing, mostly because our goal had been to see as much of the world as possible. Even still, there was plenty to be grateful about. Not only did I experience Asia for the first time, but we received the royal treatment once we were eliminated. CBS producers put us up in a posh, private resort in Thailand (complete with a large pool, massage therapists, and private chefs), where we partied literally every day for a month until the race was over. As wonderful as it was, we still longed to be in the race. That's why I call it the amazing vacation we never wanted.

In the end, the goat farmers, Josh Kilmer-Purcell and Brent Ridge of *The Fabulous Beekman Boys* fame, claimed the million-dollar prize. Even once we returned home, we couldn't tell our friends where we'd been. It was so hard not to blurt out, "Oh my God, we just went on this huge adventure!" We had to keep our mouths shut until the show premiered on September 30, 2012. Our friends, family, and Facebook fans threw their support behind us from the first episode. "We hope you win!" so many said. As we watched the first two episodes along with them, we bit our tongues and cringed inside because we already knew the outcome.

One day right in the middle of all that, we got another piece of news. I logged on to Facebook to see a press release that announced, "Adaptive snowboarding is to be part of the 2014 Paralympic Games." What?! I had to read it twice before I even showed it to Daniel. "Could this be true?" I said, my voice rising by a full octave. This announcement was completely out of the blue; none of the other organizations we'd partnered with had heard about it, either. To this day, we still don't know why the committee reversed its decision—but they did.

When we returned from Thailand, Daniel and I moved to Summit County, Colorado, the mecca for snow sports. We rented a large house at the base of Copper Mountain and opened the doors for other adaptive athletes and wounded vets who wanted to train with us that season. It was time to shift my focus from *The Amazing Race* to the real one: preparing to make the U.S. snowboarding team so I could earn my spot on the U.S. Paralympic team.

. . .

ATHLETES AREN'T BORN. They're created. Of course, some do have a build, height, or arm span that helps with athleticism, but much of what makes someone an athlete comes from habits that can be built. Like discipline in exercise. The ability to push past borders. And protein—plenty of protein.

I didn't really consider myself an "athlete" until I was thirty-three. Yes, I'd won some competitions, but in the snowboarding season of 2012, I stepped up my level of competitiveness and athleticism in a major way. In order to make one of the five spots on the U.S. snowboarding team, I needed to do well in at least four competitions. So when I moved into the place we shared in Copper Mountain, I showed up to push myself. To snowboard every single day. To adjust my legs for optimum performance. To get in the best physical shape of my life. And to triumph in as many competitions as I could.

I'd already earned that pair of golds in France, and I'd also claimed gold in New Zealand. But in both these world cups, I was barely ahead of my competition. Many of the para-snowboarders I rode against were athletes who'd trained through our organization. We'd been competing against one another for years, in part so we could bring attention to the sport. These women—most of whom were younger than me, and all of whom had a single-leg amputation—had always been right on my tail. And by the 2012 season, I was sometimes only winning by a tenth of a second. In fact, I actually lost our national competition. These women were fierce.

Even when you're competing in an international competition, you receive points that count toward a spot on the U.S. team. So with my victories abroad, I was already considered a top-ranked snowboarder. Yet in order to make the U.S. team, I needed to add competitions in Canada and Slovenia, and I got silver in both. In these races, I came in second to a force-of-nature snowboarder, Bibian Mentel of the Netherlands. That woman has set the bar for Paralympic snowboarding; she is even better than some of the male athletes, and I have major respect for her. She'd been a professional snowboarder for many years, but then after breaking her leg, she discovered she had a bone tumor that could spread to the rest of her body via her blood. So she had to have her leg amputated. She went on to regain her exact same world ranking among able-bodied snowboarders. Even after an amputation, you can choose whether to compete against able-bodied snowboarders or para-snowboarders. Bibian has triumphed at both.

I made the U.S. team, and my next goal was to make the Paralympic team. After those of us on the U.S. team went to a two-week training camp in Mount Hood, Oregon (where the snow was wet and sloppy from pouring rain, which was good preparation for learning to compete in gnarly conditions), we went on to do training camps at the Olympic Training Center in Colorado Springs, Colorado. That's when I really kicked into high gear. In addition to working with trainers at the center, I also hired my own trainer, David, in Summit County. I only know his last name as "Ass Kicker," because that's how I had him listed in my phone. He was also a trainer for CrossFit International.

My sessions were intense. David, who had tattoos up and down his muscular arms, told me, "You can come in and train with me every single day at the same time." At this point, I was 108 pounds, and most of the other female athletes I competed against were 130-plus pounds, which played in their favor because the momentum of that extra weight carried them down the course faster. If I wanted to make it onto that podium, I needed to build some muscle and gain weight. So between July 2013 and January 2014, I did everything David coached me to do. Everything.

First meal of the day: a protein shake with carbs in it, plus a few scoops of almond butter. Next, a training session that included quickly rowing for 1,000 meters on the row machine at a high intensity; then twenty pull-ups; then pushing a sled with 120 pounds of weight stacked on top of it; then explosive squats, with a 50-pound chain attached to me for building my legs and quads. I would repeat this workout five or more times per session. Once I pushed past the pain, I realized I had more strength than I ever knew. Our minds give up more quickly than our bodies do.

David's philosophy was that if you train with speed and intensity (and, thus, build fast-twitch muscle fibers), you'll compete with speed and intensity. That's why most of our exercises were 30 seconds of all-out pushing, then 30 seconds of rest, followed by another 30 seconds of explosive movement. We also did toes-to-rings: I hung from a gymnast ring, kept my body straight, then lifted my toes up through the rings. I did that in sets of fifteen. We changed the workouts daily. By the end, I was wiped. Each week, I took two days off from David to let my muscles recover, and I road cycled instead.

Within thirty minutes after weight training, it's good to eat protein because it feeds your muscles. So after my session, I'd go home and have six egg whites along with sweet potatoes. Since I was also trying to put on pounds, I added fat to a lot of what I ate. For instance, I'd put calorie-dense coconut butter on top of my sweet potatoes. In the afternoons, I drank another protein shake, and maybe goat's milk, which contains a lot of amino acids. Then for dinner, I had more chicken or fish and plenty of vegetables, or I'd sometimes finish the night off with another protein shake. I'd go to bed dreaming of breakfast the next day. That's how ravenous these workouts made me. Every morning, I'd wake up, throw on my legs, and practically run to the kitchen. I was constantly eating. At many points during a day, I was tempted to open the fridge, grab a whole chicken, and start eating right off the carcass.

I put on twelve pounds over six months. And they weren't just pounds; they were solid muscle. My body had never been so toned. For the first time in my life, I had a six-pack. Because all my extra weight was muscle, I never even went up in pant size. I just looked much better in the pants I already had. That's amazing to me, because when I was younger, I'd always been scared to train with weights. I didn't want to bulk up. But I wasn't bulky at all. In fact, I'd never felt better about my body. I was strong. I was capable. I was fit. And every night just before I drifted off to sleep, I could actually visualize myself on that medal podium.

CHAPTER 16

New Roles

"One of the secrets to life is to make stepping stones
out of stumbling blocks."

—JACK PENN

In October 2012, I got an email from Matthew Vaughn, the celebrated British film director who did *X-Men*. For his upcoming action-comedy Warner Bros. film *Kingsman: The Secret Service*, Matthew had been searching for an actor who could play the character of Gazelle, a bad-ass assassin with bionic legs. Matthew's search had led him to me. Very exciting.

I'd been out there enough in the media that people were starting to take notice of me, and I was grateful for that. In addition to *What's Bugging Seth* and that Madonna video, I also did a 2008 project with rocker-turned-photographer Nikki Sixx of Mötley Crüe. He photographed me wearing custom legs that looked like metal ice picks; the photo series, titled "Amy in Wonderland," ended up in his *New York Times* bestselling book *This Is Going to*

Hurt. So when Matthew approached me, I saw it as another chance to grow my acting career, as well as to present my legs not as clunky steel parts to be hidden, but as sleek accessories I wore with pride.

By this time, I'd hired an agent—Patrick Quinn in Chicago. So Patrick wrote back to Matthew on my behalf. "Amy would love to try out for the role," he explained, "but I need to know the filming schedule. She's training for the Paralympics, and there's no point in her auditioning if the shoot schedule will conflict. Let me know." Thankfully, the film would be shot that same fall in London, which meant I could squeeze it in, or at least try. So I sent in the audition tape. They loved the tape and offered to fly me to London for three days to do an in-studio audition and some training with their martial arts team. If there was any double-amputee woman in the world who could do roundhouse kicks on two running blades, I wanted to be that woman.

They flew me first-class. I drank champagne and savored filet mignon. I felt so special, being jetted overseas on my first trip to London to audition for a role with one of the most well-regarded studios in the world. I couldn't help but think about all those years when I'd sat around bonfires with my friends in the desert, hoping and dreaming and imagining that I'd one day get to discover faraway lands.

Around ten o'clock on the morning of the meeting, a black car picked me up and took me to the two-hundred-acre studio in Leavesden. I looked out my window to see "Warner Bros. Studios" in large silver letters on the front of the building. *I can't even believe I'm here.* Matthew himself came out to greet me. "Hello, Amy," he said, extending his hand. He was very friendly. "I'm glad you could come out." After some small talk, Matthew handed me off to one of his producers for an "interview," though the whole thing was casual. He pulled up a chair for both of us, and we sat down to chitchat.

"We loved what we saw in your audition tape," said the producer. "We just have to be sure you can do what's physically demanded for this role. It's a lot of martial arts." *Bring it on,* I thought. The producer explained that in this film adaptation of the Mark Millar and David Gibbons spy comic book series, Gazelle's running-blade legs would turn into Samurai swords. "She'll do roundhouse kicks and slice people's heads off," he said. I paused. "Well, I'm a snowboarder," I said, "and honestly, my balance is probably better than any double-leg amputee in the world. I think I can do this." He nodded and smiled, as if to say, "We'll see." He went on to tell me about the cast. For the role of the head assassin, a major actor had already signed on—Samuel Jackson.

He handed me the script. "Read this today," he said. "This afternoon, we'll go through all your scenes." The script was thick and heavy. *"Today?"* I said. "Yes, today," he said. "Why don't you go have some lunch, read over everything, and we'll see you back here in a few hours." Before I left, Matthew circled back and took me to meet his wife, supermodel Claudia Schiffer. She had on zero makeup and still looked flawless. She wore a one-piece jumper and tall wedges. She was even more stunning and gracious in person than she'd been when I saw her in the pages of *Vogue*. "I'll be developing the look of this character, and I've already got some ideas," she said after we'd chatted for a few minutes. "Let me walk you over to wardrobe so they can take your measurements." I thought, *Don't I still have to audition for the part?* But of course, I went with it.

184 ॐ Amy Purdy

Back at my hotel over tea and dessert, I spent the next two hours leafing through the script and making some quick notes on the kinds of choices my character would make. Frankly, that's all I had time to do. When I returned to the studio, the producer led me to the audition room. Matthew was already there. "I'll be standing in as Valentine, the lead villain who plays opposite Gazelle," he told me. *I should've studied the script better.* Moments later, we launched right into the first scene.

I fumbled a line. My voice shook a little. I was rusty. It had been years since I last acted, but thank goodness I at least had that experience to pull from. I got through it and felt okay about it, unlike my first scene of the *Seth* movie. "So, we have some work to do here," the producer said afterward. "Let's take it from the top." We went through the scene again, which went much better. "Very good," Matthew said. "Now we just need to make sure you can do the martial arts."

The producer took me over to this big warehouse. There I met a crew of amazing martial arts guys; one of them had even trained Jackie Chan. "Let's see what you've got," he said. Right there in front of them, I swapped my walking legs for my running blades. One of the guys handed me a fake gun. "Here's what we want you to do," he said. He then showed me this whole routine in which I'd somersault, get up on one knee, roll onto the other knee, and point the gun toward one of the guys. I nailed it. "That was spectacular," he told me. That felt good.

Afterward, Matthew asked me to extend my time there. "How about if you to stay an additional week so we can set you up with an acting coach to develop the character?" I agreed. For the next several days, I met with this brilliant coach named Katie. The techniques I learned helped me to bring my character to life. I loved it. Then at the end of that additional week, Matthew requested that I stay another three weeks. "I'm ninety-nine-point-nine percent sure you have this part," he said. "We just need the studio to agree, so you might as well continue to build the character with Katie and train, as well as figure out if we can make your snowboard training schedule work with our filming schedule." That sounded like a great plan.

Once that training was complete, I did a final audition. "Perfect—beautiful!" said Matthew after I'd said my last line. Katie, who'd been observing, came over and whispered, "That was killer." I'd already begun working out a possible schedule in my head. Patrick had told me that if I got the role, I'd be shooting for several weeks in London between November 2013 and January 16, 2014. From London, I'd have to find a way to fit in some competitions in order to rack up enough points toward making the Paralympic team, which included a mandatory world cup event on January 18. And during any downtime on the filming, I could take a quick flight over to Austria and keep up with my snowboard training. *Done.*

Right after that final audition, I was planning to fly home, but then Matthew called me with one last request.

"I just heard Sam Jackson will be here in two days," he said. "Can you stay? I want you guys to go through the script together."

"Sure," I said. I'd already been there a whole month. What was two more days? I knew I'd be cutting it very close to the start of my upcoming camp, but I really wanted this role. And I definitely wanted to meet Sam.

Sam arrived the next day. The producers, Matthew, and I all

met at his hotel lobby and walked up to his suite. The room was fancy, and the Warner Bros. team had already filled it with racks of outfits so Sam could begin looking through his wardrobe options. Seconds after we entered, Sam walked around the corner and warmly greeted Matthew and the others. "Hey, man!" he said. "Great to see you." He then turned toward me, and I confidently stretched my hand in his direction. "We don't shake hands around here!" Sam said with that booming voice and infectious laugh of his. "We hug!" We embraced, and then we all sat down together.

By this point, I knew my character inside and out, and I basically showed up that day *as* Gazelle. Sam, on the other hand, had little idea who his character was. He hadn't yet had a chance to study the script and develop the role. He flipped through it as we sat.

"Okay," he said to Matthew, "so what scene are we starting with?"

"We'll start with the scene where you two are at the computer together," Matthew responded.

"Which scene is that?" asked Sam.

I piped in: "It's scene fifty-three—on page one fifty-eight."

Sam smiled. "Whoa, you got this down, don't you!" he said, flipping over to the page where I'd directed.

We stood and set up the scene, and right away it was clear that Sam had made a choice about how he'd play Valentine, a character who, as a kid, was recruited from his tough street life to become part of a secret spy organization. Sam had the first line, and he delivered it with this goofy lisp! "You didn't expect that, now did you?" he said, breaking out of character for a moment. I smiled. I then went on to deliver my first line, and I brought all the power and presence to that delivery that Katie and I had rehearsed. "Wow, now I didn't expect that from *your* character!" said Sam. On paper, Gazelle, the assistant to Valentine, could be interpreted as the less powerful of the two. But after delving into the character, I'd interpreted her the way I saw her—as a woman in full control.

"Okay, okay," said Sam, "I see how you're playing things." We did another back-and-forth—and afterward, he said, "Damn, girl—you're good." Sam and I hugged once more, and then we left.

On the way out, Matthew said to me, "This couldn't have gone better. Now we just need to figure out the exact filming schedule and work out all the contract details with your agent. But you can start packing your stuff. We'll need you back here in two weeks." On my car ride to the airport, I was on the highest high. *I just worked with Sam Jackson and got a kick-ass part in a major film!* I thought. I boarded another first-class flight and stared dreamily out the window as the wheels lifted off the ground.

Once home, I spent two whole days with Daniel—some much-needed R&R. I then began my training camp and had one day to pack after that. What would I even *take*? I didn't know for sure, yet I somehow quickly filled three huge bags. When you have multiple sets of legs to pack, that's often the way it goes; plus I was taking all my snowboard gear.

"I'd love it if you could fly over to London at some point," I told Daniel.

"That would be awesome," he said. "This last trip, it felt like you were gone *forever*—I'd love to see you at least once this time around."

Meanwhile, the film's producers had arranged for me to fly down to Florida and get some work done on my legs. I did that. In fact, on my way back to London a couple of weeks later, I was to leave directly from Orlando. The studio booked my plane ticket for a Saturday, and by that Friday, I was completely ready.

That evening, my cell rang. It was Patrick. "I have some bad news," he said.

"What?" I said. I could feel the blood draining from my face.

"You've been cut from the film," he told me.

I went silent. "What do you mean I've been cut?" I finally said, barely even able to get the sentence out.

"Well," he said, "someone from the studio, a person I'd never even talked to, called up and said they'd decided to let you go."

I was stunned. "But why?" I said.

"He mentioned a conflict with your snowboard training and their insurance policy. If you were to get injured, they wouldn't even have a stunt double."

"But I just talked to one of the producers last night!" I said. "How did this just suddenly come up?"

Patrick sighed. "I really don't know." Later, I did get a call from a producer. He told me he'd battled all weekend with the studio, but ultimately, the studio won.

The following afternoon, I talked with Stan, my prosthetist. I told him my sad news. And naturally, because he'd worked so hard to get my legs ready, he was just as disappointed as I was. "Well, Amy," he said, "there's gotta be something bigger around the corner for you. You'll just have to wait and see."

I thought, *What else could be bigger than starring in a movie with Sam Jackson? A movie where the character seemed made for me? This was my opportunity to mix my athletic skills with my acting skills. Whatever comes next couldn't be as amazing.*

But then again, I told myself, maybe Stan was right. Maybe his words coincided with that inkling I'd had for years. I couldn't imagine what could be "bigger" than a major Warner Bros. film. But perhaps it could be just a stepping-stone to something more.

I THREW MYSELF back into snowboard training. About a month into that, Patrick forwarded me an email from Deena Katz, a senior talent producer at *Dancing with the Stars*—the long-running celebrity dance competition on ABC. "We'd like to invite you to be on Season 18 of the show," read the email. "If this is an opportunity that interests you, please call us." She listed her number. A day later, I was on a conference call with Deena and two other producers.

"Do you have any dance experience?" Deena asked.

"Not much," I admitted, "but I thoroughly love to dance." Just weeks before this call, I'd told Daniel I wanted to try a ballroom dancing class, and that maybe the two of us could take a salsa or tango class after the Paralympics were over. "I at least have rhythm," I told Deena. "This could be fun."

"If this works out," she said, "do you think you could come out to L.A. for a couple of days and meet your dance partner?" She suggested a date.

"That's right at the peak of my training for the Paralympics," I told her. "But I could make this work if my partner came here to Colorado to meet me."

"We'll see what we can do," said Deena. "We'll circle back once we figure out what we can do." We hung up.

Small confession: Though I'd heard plenty about *Dancing*

with the Stars, I'd only caught a few episodes here and there. Frankly, I'd been a little busy since the show first began airing back in 2005, the same year Daniel and I started AAS. So after Deena's call, I watched several episodes of the show online. In the space of a few hours, I'd gone from "This could be fun" to both terrified and excited all at once.

That feeling didn't last. A couple of days later in talking with Deena, Patrick heard that the eighteenth season's first episode would air on March 17, 2014, just days after the Paralympic snowboard events were scheduled to get under way. Since rehearsals would have to begin weeks before the premiere, it didn't look like it could work. I'd hardly had a chance to let the good news sink in, and it was already disappearing. "Can you just turn it down now and tell them I'll do it in the fall?" I said to Patrick. "It's going to be nearly impossible for me to squeeze it in now." So Patrick delivered that message to Deena. And I moved on.

NOVEMBER 2013: TIME for me to refocus on making the U.S. Paralympic team. As a way to earn points and secure a spot for myself, I'd signed on for several races in the Netherlands, Copper Mountain, Canada, and Spain. By this time, I already had several big sponsors paying for my races. Even before the athletic teams are fully in place, sponsors can attend an Olympic summit at which they decide whom they'll put their dollars behind. Thankfully, Patrick had arranged for me to attend that summit, and I was one of only a few of Olympic hopefuls there. Because of my exposure through TED, the fact that I could speak well, and their curiosity about this new Paralympic sport, a slew of sponsors got behind me. Toyota had stood behind me well before the Paralympics were even a possibility. Other companies like Kelloggs, Coca-Cola, Procter and Gamble, and The Hartford also came on board to support me. This was huge, because many of the sponsors had not previously stepped forward to support Paralympians in the same way that they had Olympians. What a blessing. So I was all set with sponsorships—I just needed to do well enough in my remaining races to actually make it to Sochi.

Before the final races, I'd spent months searching for just the right snowboarding legs. That fall, I had a breakthrough. It came in the form of a phone call from a friend who'd built his own snowboarding foot when he couldn't find one he liked.

"I really want you to try out this foot," he said. "It may be amazing for what you're doing with snowboarding because it's got an adjustable air shock in it. It keeps your foot flat, but at the same time, it has a bend to it, so that you can actually engage your knee." I told him I'd give it a try. That's what I love about this community: We're doers. If something hasn't been made, we make it.

The moment I put on the foot, I thought, *This is a game-changer.* The feet seemed to work best if I only wore one of them, the one on my back foot. That's because you do more bending with that leg while you're snowboarding. So I kept my original foot in the front, which was from my sponsor Freedom Innovations; I switched the back one to the new foot. Right away, I noticed a difference in my overall riding. My toe edge became much cleaner and sharper; in fact, the toe edge seemed even better than it had been when I was on my real legs. I decided to try it at the upcoming world cup in the Netherlands, but I didn't tell my coach that I'd made the change. I didn't want him to try to talk me out of it. I knew what worked for me.

As it turns out, I was right. In that world cup, I still came in second to Bibian—but I got closer to her time than ever before! In that race, I also noticed that some of the women I'd competed against previously had gotten better, stronger, faster. I might've upped my game, but so had they, and while I did manage to get a silver, they were right on my behind. That made me even more thrilled that I'd gotten this foot. They all had one good leg. And I now had one great foot to help equalize the field.

Back at home, I became nearly obsessed with fine-tuning my feet. Yes, the new foot was great, but even still, I spent hours micro-adjusting both feet, just to be sure they worked well in various conditions, from powder to slush and ice. By the time two back-to-back world cups in Copper Mountain rolled around in January 2014, I felt more ready than ever. This race was happening on my home mountain. I really wanted to finish with a gold.

I took my spot in the start gate for a practice run on the day before the race. I came out in a low tuck ahead of the others. *This is exactly what I've been training for—good.* This particular course was really fast, steep, and icy. I made it over three steep rollers and carved a sharp heel-side edge around the first berm. *My legs and training are paying off.* Picking up major speed, I went around a toe-side berm. That's when the g-forces kicked in, and—*squish!*—my foot completely collapsed beneath me. As the other riders whizzed by, I somehow made it through the rest of the course. In a panic, I whipped out my tools to see if I could adjust that back foot. I pumped up the toe shock with air. I then tried another practice run, and it did not go much better. *Shit.*

I spent the whole rest of that day and the next morning trying to fix that foot. If you think I was obsessive before, I turned into an absolute madwoman at this point. "You'll figure it out," Daniel told me, in an attempt to be encouraging. In frustration with trying to fix it myself, I finally admitted to my coach that I'd switched my foot. He was irritated, both that I had hidden the change, and that I was fooling around with my equipment so close to the competition season. He didn't say a whole lot when I told him, but his facial expression said it all: "You've got twenty-four hours to figure it out." The other racers—many of whom had seemed intimidated by me over the years—had seen me struggling in the practice runs, so the pressure was on. They spotted an opening to take me down.

The next day, I got into my position in the starting gate. I launched off a Wu Tang, a vertical jump shaped like the wall of a halfpipe. *Good*. But around every single toe edge, I lost major speed. My toe edges felt like they were melting into butter. Disappointed, I struggled to even finish the race. I came in fifth place. Yes, fifth. It was the first world cup in four years at which I'd missed making the podium. When I crossed the finish line, some of the other competitors were high-fiving one another. "You guys were *fast*," I said, congratulating them. "Great job." Now, mind you, none of these girls had won the race. Bibian, as usual, had been unstoppable and claimed gold. But for these other riders, simply outracing me was enough reason to celebrate. "Yes!" I heard one of them say. "We finally got her!"

Not only had they beat me, but I now had a big target on my back. They'd proven that I could be taken out, even on my home mountain. It didn't help that a few of my huge sponsors for the upcoming Paralympics had been there to witness my humiliating mechanical failure. Not good for business. I had gotten my ass kicked by athletes who'd never even previously medaled. That night, I stayed up for hours, fiddling with that foot.

My race the following day was better, but not by much. I fought a little harder and came in fourth place instead of fifth. Then two days later, we were off to Big White Mountain in Canada for another competition. I decided that as much potential as that new foot had, I didn't have enough time to figure it out and I couldn't take a chance. So I went back to using both my original feet. Though they didn't have the ankle motion of the new foot, at least those feet had consistently put me in second place. There must have been something to my theory, because I upgraded my position and came in third place. It was as if I'd said, "That's right, ladies. I'm working my way back up!" Then, in the second race, I reclaimed my second-place spot on the podium. After that competition in Canada, I picked up enough points to reach my goal—I'd made the 2014 Paralympic Team. *Yes.*

I didn't even have to compete in the final world cup in La Molina, Spain, but I did anyway, just for practice. The course was a fun one, lots of berms and fast rollers and one really steep toe-side turn. I did my first practice run. It went very well. So in my second practice run, I opened up wide and really let myself go. I went around a heel-side turn, over a roller, onto my toe-side turn, but my toe edge slipped, the nose of my board clipped the safety netting, and . . . I flew head over heels three times, smacking my forehead against the poles that held up the netting! My whole body went tumbling like a rag doll and I ended up face-down in the snow.

Travis McClain, the former pro snowboarder and our assistant coach, bolted to where I lay. "Oh my God, can you hear me, Amy?!" he shouted, leaning over me. I couldn't catch my breath long enough to respond. "It's my damn toes," I finally muttered with a groan. "It's that stupid toe edge." He helped me to my feet and I stumbled to the sidelines. I was rattled, but once I was upright, I seemed physically okay. "I'm not even going to show you the video of that crash," my coach told me later that day. "Please just put this out of your mind."

The next morning, I awakened with major whiplash. My forehead was bruised. My back was aching in three places. When you become a competitive snowboarder, that's what you sign up for. You can't play it too safe with a run. You either have to commit and go for it, or you should probably just go home. It's often when you do hold back—when you hesitate and second-guess yourself with every move—that you end up hurting yourself. So even with all the pain I was in, I didn't regret my choice to go for it. I took a chance. I'd learned that no reward comes without risk.

Later that day in La Molina, I showed up to compete, despite my aches. I put it all on the line with every turn and toe edge, and I won yet another world cup silver. But then as I got into the start gates for my second race, my whole body went numb. Suddenly I couldn't move my head. My neck throbbed. My coach rushed me over to the clinic. "Maybe you broke something yesterday and didn't know it," he said. The doctor took some X-rays and a few minutes later, he came in with the results. "Nothing looks broken," he said. "What you're feeling is a muscle spasm from the whiplash. You should be fine once the spasm relaxes." Or so he thought.

CHAPTER 17

Sochi

"Each of us has a fire in our hearts for something.
It's our goal in life to find it and keep it lit."

—MARY LOU RETTON

Three weeks before the Sochi games, I received another email from Deena at *Dancing with the Stars*. This time, her invitation was official. She'd found a way to work with my schedule. "We can come to you," she told me by phone, explaining that the show would arrange for my dance partner, along with a producer, to first meet me in Colorado; my partner could then fly all the way to Sochi so we could prepare our first dance. "We'd really love to have you on during this spring season."

The timing would be tight. There'd be just three days between my Paralympic race and the premiere episode, but I figured *Why not? It will be nice to have something to jump into after the Paralympics.* And at this point, I was in the best shape of my life. So I signed on. Later that day, I called my sister to share the good news. "Oh my God, I hope you get Derek Hough as your partner!" she yelled. I'd heard of Derek, but frankly, since I hadn't really followed the show, I couldn't quite remember which one he was. "He's *so* cute," Crystal went on, "and he's won the most mirror ball trophies. He's a genius!" Thanks and noted.

In the days leading up to Sochi, the other U.S. team members and I traveled to Aspen for one final training camp. Early one morning, I sat up in bed and the room began to spin horribly.

"Oh my God, something's wrong!" I yelled.

My roommate bolted in. "What's going on, Amy!?"

"I'm spinning!" I said, pressing my palms to the sides of my head. Then not even two seconds later, the spinning came to a halt. And by the time we all gathered for breakfast, I felt fine. But then later that day while I was training, it happened again.

My coach sent me to a doctor, who diagnosed me with benign paroxysmal positional vertigo. "BPPV develops when the inner-ear crystals that help your body determine the direction of gravity come loose," he explained. "When you move your head in a certain direction, or you sit up and down, a brief episode of vertigo suddenly hits. The condition is often caused by head trauma." As in that brain-spinning crash I'd survived in Spain. The doctor concluded that even with therapy, the condition could take anywhere from a few days to several months to treat. In other words, I might be dizzy through Russia and *Dancing with the Stars*. Great.

I didn't finish the camp. Instead, I frantically searched the Internet to find a therapist who could get these crazy ear crystals back into place. I found someone. So that night, I drove home to Summit County, Colorado, to see a physical therapist who moved my head side to side and around in a way that was supposed to alleviate the vertigo. It didn't work. One day after that, the producer from *Dancing with the Stars* (*DWTS*) showed up so we could begin. My agent had told me we'd be meeting for the first time that day, but I'd been so focused on my training and this vertigo crisis that I hadn't remembered. Besides that, at this point I had learned to not get overly excited about opportunities until I knew for sure they were happening. Part of me had never believed that *DWTS* would actually happen, just as that Madonna video and Sam Jackson movie had fallen through, too.

The *DWTS* team had rented a local dance studio where I was to meet the producer and then be introduced to my dance partner. That morning, I showed up to the studio feeling half dazed. I'd thrown on a yellow beanie cap (it was snowing outside and plus my hair was a little wild that morning), a flannel shirt, leggings, and my snow boots. When I arrived, a cameraman was already in place. He pointed the camera toward me—no time for lip gloss. "Hello, Amy!" said the producer, walking toward me. "How excited are you to be on *Dancing with the Stars*?"

I paused. "Well, I'm excited . . . yeah," I said. *Is this really happening?* I thought.

"If you could choose anyone as your dance partner, whom would you choose?" he asked.

I recalled what Crystal had told me. "Derek," I told him. I only said his first name because I didn't yet know how to pronounce his last name. Embarrassing.

"Well, I'm going to step inside the studio," said the producer, "and when I yell for you, please walk in and meet your partner."

The producer called out to me, and I walked up to the door and pushed it open. The cameraman was filming me. When I walked into the tiny, mirrored studio, this adorable blond guy with a huge smile stood right in front of me. He wore a tight-fitting thermal top and jeans. *Holy shit—I actually got Derek.*

"Hi!" he said, embracing me enthusiastically. He was very high-energy. "I'm Derek Hough."

In my head, I noted how he pronounced his last name— rhymes with *tough*. "Great to finally meet you!" I said, my voice shaking. *Oh my God—this* is *really happening.* In that moment, I felt a shot of dizziness and swayed a bit.

"You okay?" he asked.

"Yes, I'm fine," I lied. "I'm just getting over a light concussion." I hadn't said a word to anyone at *DWTS* about my vertigo; the last thing I needed was anyone second-guessing whether I could get through the show.

Before jumping in, Derek and I talked a bit. "What made you want to do the show?" he asked.

"I think it's a great departure from what I've been doing," I said. "I wanted a new challenge. And I wanted to see what's possible." I motioned down toward my legs. "To be honest, I have no idea what I'm capable of with dancing. I've never done anything like this before."

Right then, he took me by both my hands and looked directly at me. "Look," he said, "I wasn't even planning to come back to the show this season. I've already won the mirror ball plenty of times, and I'm at a new place in life. I want to be a part of something bigger, something more meaningful and fulfilling. That's why when the producers told me about your story, I said, 'I absolutely have to come back for this.' So let's just figure this thing out together, babe. We're here to defy the odds. You ready?"

I smiled, and we high-fived. "Let's start by getting those things off," said Derek, pointing toward my snow boots. He leaned down and began helping me remove them. *Such a gentleman.* I loved his very assertive, take-charge energy.

Derek brought my dance shoes, a pair of basic, nude-colored, two-inch practice heels that the producers had gotten once they'd confirmed my size. I sat, and Derek strapped on my dance shoes one at a time, catching his first up-close look at these metal legs of mine. "Wow, these are *cool*," he said as he fastened a buckle. "I can't wait to see what we can do." I stood.

"Let's just play around a bit," he said. "Put your hand on your hip." I placed it there, not at all confident about my ability to handle whatever was coming next. "Okay, that's fine," said Derek, scanning the way I held my body, as if he was taking some mental notes. "We're just going to loosen up and have fun. Let's try a couple of cha-cha moves," he said. He demonstrated for me, and I tried to follow along, but my movements were stiff and uncertain. In fact, in our first few minutes together, I felt shy. I was more out of my element than I'd expected.

"You're doing fine," Derek said, trying to reassure me, but I could tell the wheels were turning in his head. "Remember, we're just playing right now. Do you have any dance experience?"

"Well," I said, "I used to clog dance when I was twelve." We both laughed.

"Fantastic. Show me!" he said. I started to dance and even let out a "Woo-hoo!" as I kicked my knee up toward my chest. We both laughed. He seemed impressed with how well I could move around.

"We might be able to incorporate that somewhere," he said. "What other kinds of dancing do you know how to do?"

I started shaking my head like the girl in the *Flashdance* movie, a dance I'd recently done at a friend's eighties party.

"Okay, so don't ever do *that again!*" he said, laughing. "Do you know how to do the grapevine?" I nodded and showed him. I had those down because we used to do them in our country clog dances when I was a kid.

"Oh my God," he said, "that was so beautiful that I could just *kiss* you right now!" He threw his arms around me for a hug.

Over the course of our two hours of dancing, I loosened up. *I like this guy,* I thought. *He's fun and has the same figure-it-out attitude that I do.* My vertigo did kick in a few times, but I assured Derek that I was fine. "It's no big deal," I said, secretly worried. He promised we'd work around it.

"The other teams have close to three weeks to learn their first dance," he told me as we wrapped up the first session. "We'll practice here for another two hours tomorrow, and then I'll be back on a plane. After that, I guess I'll see you in Sochi, right?" I nodded. I was still getting used to the idea that this whole thing was happening.

Once home, I did more research on Derek. I pulled up a couple of YouTube videos of his Season 16 dances with country music star Kellie Pickler, and I couldn't believe how fast some of their dance steps were! She also had these amazing lines and beautiful pointed toes in many of the dances. My heart sank. Could I really do this? I called Patrick. "What if my legs can't handle this? What if I make a fool out of myself? And what if I can't move my feet fast enough to keep up with Derek?"

"All you have to worry about is not being the first contestant eliminated," he said. "Then you'll at least be on there for two weeks, and that itself is an accomplishment." It was a good point, and took some pressure off. I didn't have to win; I just had to get through week one. After that second day of rehearsal with Derek, I left for Russia.

OUR FLIGHT TO Sochi was chartered. On the way, our team stopped at the Olympic processing center in Munich to pick up our official Team USA gear. When we arrived in Sochi, I stared out the window for the entire ride from the airport to the Olympic Village. I'd actually visited Sochi once the year before; I'd been part of a delegation of athletes sent to test the runs and snow conditions. This time around, I was shocked by how much different the place looked. In less than twelve months, it had gone from a town "under construction" to a full-fledged resort area with vast new buildings all around.

Pulling into the Olympic Village felt so surreal. *I can't believe I'm actually here.* After years of work to make this experience happen, it felt amazing to just be in Russia. At the very moment we arrived, news broke that I was on the upcoming cast of *Dancing with the Stars*. My phone, which had been sitting quietly in my lap, suddenly began buzzing with Twitter messages. I silenced it. When I looked at it again later, all my social media accounts had exploded! Two of the biggest and most exciting opportunities of my life were happening at the exact same time, and the level of gratitude I felt was overwhelming. When I got off the bus, I looked up to the sky and whispered, "Thank you." We checked into our rooms, which were bare-bones—just a couple of twin beds and an Ikea-like wardrobe. This would be our home for two weeks.

The Olympic Village really is its own little town. Each country's athletes stayed in its own building. In the village center, a whole row of every country's flags flew overhead—it was beautiful. Right there on campus, we had a twenty-four-hour cafeteria with all the food any athlete would want. We also had a dentist. A bank. A movie theater. A hair salon. Even a prosthetic shop. It was all nestled right alongside the base of the resort near the mountain. From the village, we could already see that the snow conditions weren't great. Actually, we'd realized that ahead of time, because from Colorado, we'd closely watched the Winter Olympics on television in February. Despite our fears about the snow, we were all amazed to be there, not only for ourselves, but for our sport. On this trip, we'd be making history: Para-snowboarding would be represented at the games for the very first time, a major landmark.

Every morning, we jumped on a shuttle that took us to the mountain, where we snowboarded for four hours. The snow was even worse than we'd first thought. It felt almost like quicksand in some spots, hard and icy in others, and a mixture of natural and man-made snow. Overall, I'd describe the snow as very mashed-potatoey, and that had a lot to with the humidity; the average daytime temperature hovered around 50 degrees, thanks to Sochi's low latitude and its position right near the Black Sea. After a couple runs we realized we'd be dealing with changing conditions. From one run to the next, the snow would turn from slick to slushy, making it nearly impossible to hold on to a toe edge. "Everything I've taught you about snowboarding over the last two years—throw out the window," said Miah, my coach, when he saw the snow's ever-changing conditions. "This is not snowboarding. This is more like surfing."

Our racecourse hadn't been set up ahead of time, so every day we did warm-up runs and drill techniques to carve efficiently through the difficult snow. On that first day, literally every one of us ended up with our faces planted into the ground! With such terrible snow, we had to practice shifting our weight differently, just to keep from sinking into the snow. That afternoon, I came back to the village with bruises down my legs, which had rarely happened to me in practice back home. Yet I was grateful that at least my vertigo hadn't seemed to bother me out on the mountain. As for my beat-up legs, there was a physical therapy room where we could go and wrap our legs in ice compressors; that took away all the bruising. I went there just about every afternoon. I needed to be sure my legs stayed strong, both for dancing and for riding.

In the days leading right up to the race, our course took shape right before our eyes, and the view wasn't a very good one. It was extremely steep and narrow, different from the course the Olympic snowboarders had ridden; in part, the officials had chosen to put us on this part of the mountain because the end of this course was close to a stadium seating venue where hundreds of onlookers could easily see the athletes cross the finish line. Since our sport was brand-new, there'd be media wanting to cover us.

On the one hand, it was awesome to have such major press attention for Adaptive Snowboard Cross; that's part of what Daniel and I had been working so hard toward. We'd taken ownership of this sport, along with a handful of our other teammates; we all wanted it to look really good both for those gathered, and for those who watched from afar. But from the standpoint of the race, the steepness would make this run extremely difficult to manage. You don't want a course that's too steep, because there are jumps and berms (a wall of snow built up in a corner) to navigate along the way, and the steepness pulls you down with too much speed. "This looks *nothing* like we'd imagined our course would look," my teammates and I kept saying to each other. When you think of the Olympics, you dream that you'll be on the biggest, best-constructed courses there is. But this course wasn't it.

Considering the conditions, I rode pretty well in my practices. Day by day, I even crept closer to Bibian's time. I always aim to make every run my very best—and never would that be more true than in Sochi. But once I saw that course and realized what we were all up against, I knew it would come down to making fewer mistakes than my competitors, focusing on the things I *could* control, and doing whatever I had to do to get across the finish line ahead of the others.

In the mornings, I trained, and in the afternoons, I danced. By the time Derek arrived in Sochi, I'd gone from "What's this guy's last name?" to feeling completely blessed to be paired with a creative force that the whole world seemed to already be in love with. With his coaching, maybe I could do better than just avoid elimination, and actually stay in for a few weeks. Maybe I could stay in it for at least three weeks. I'd have to see how my legs held up. In our short time together, we started our cha-cha—and in the end, we just hoped for the best. Then for the four days leading right up to my race, I put dancing aside and focused on what I'd come there for—to try for a podium finish.

RACE DAY ARRIVED: March 14, 2014. My alarm went off at 5:15 A.M. I sat up, rubbed my eyes, and looked out the window at the sun rising over the Sochi peaks. I'd wanted to get up early so I could get in a workout, even if only for a few minutes. All week, my coach had been saying, "Race day is just another practice day. There's just a little added pressure. Do exactly what you do in practice." But it definitely didn't feel like just another day. It felt like the culmination of nearly a decade of serious work, not to mention the big debut of our sport. I couldn't believe it was finally here.

"You're up," said Megan, my roommate and teammate. She stretched and yawned.

"Yeah, I'm going to head down and squeeze in a little Spin cycle," I told her. There wouldn't be much time for that or breakfast: We'd all been told to be at the top of the mountain by 7:30 A.M. in order to test the snow before the race. We'd actually pushed for the race to be as early in the day as possible. We thought cooler weather might help with the snow conditions. Or at least we hoped it would.

Straight from the gym, I walked over to get something to eat at the village cafeteria. I ordered the same breakfast I'd had just about every day since I'd arrived: eggs, and these amazing crepes filled with peanut butter and maple syrup and the high-fat Russian baked yogurt. I was trying to keep weight on as much as possible. One of my teammates saw me from across the cafeteria and waved. "You ready?" she called out, walking toward me. "I'm always ready," I said. "Let's just pray the snow's in good shape today." "It just started snowing a little now," she said. "Maybe the fresh powder will help." We both nodded.

As I sat and picked over my plate, I put in my earphones and listened to "Madness" by Muse, one of the favorites for keeping my adrenaline and nerves in check before a race. All season, I'd been experimenting with the ritual of using music to focus my energy. I ate a few bites of the crepe but couldn't finish everything on my plate; the nerves had already gotten to me. I lingered there for a moment and just let the music wash over me.

I returned to my room and dressed. On my way over to the lift, Daniel—who'd flown in for the race itself, but who hadn't been able to visit me in the village—called me on my cell phone. "How are you?" he said. "I'm feeling pretty good, actually," I said, glancing up to see for myself the snowflakes descending. "Looks like the gods are with us today," I said. "We've all trained. We've done the work. We're ready. And now we just have to go out and do our very best." "And you will," Daniel said. "I know you're gonna kick ass."

By 7:15, most of us had already gathered at the chairlift, including my coach. "Remember, ladies," he said, "it's just another day of practice." We loaded into the lift, and on our way up, I looked down across the mountain. Through the light fog, I spotted the course workers, who'd been up before daybreak, prepping the course. As we gradually ascended, the mountain seemed so still, the same stillness I'd fallen in love with on my very first run in Brian Head with my guy friends all those years before. From Brian Head, Utah, to Sochi, Russia, by way of these two bionic legs. Few would have predicted that my journey would bring me all the way here.

By then, we all knew the official rules of the race. We'd get a practice run, plus three actual runs. The slowest of the three times would be dropped, and the remaining two would be averaged to determine a victory. I wanted to punctuate the season and make this Paralympic debut my best riding ever. But with the steepness of the hill, my main mission was to keep things steady, and then open wide with full speed once I moved toward the end of the course.

I prepared for my practice run. The minute I pulled out of the gate, I immediately noticed that the conditions had changed yet again. The snow had become mushy and sticky. As I carved my way around a berm, the snow was inconsistent. I would hit slush, which slowed me down, and then I'd hit hard ice. The combination of those two things made for a bumpy ride. I quickly realized I could only have one goal for this entire race: I needed to stay *upright*. My strategy would be to look for areas where I could check my speed so I could stay in control. Not as inspiring a goal as trying to outdo my best time, but sometimes staying competitive is about being flexible and adapting to changes.

As I stood in the start gates for my first run I thought, *Wow, this is it.* Years of hard work for this one moment. I wanted my first run to be a safety run; it was best to get a solid time in without falling, and then pick up the pace in the second run. I inhaled deeply and visualized myself going down the course perfectly. Visualizing has always been a great tool for me, both in competition and in life. I mapped out the course in my mind and envisioned exactly what my body would do at every turn.

I took off! I nailed five back-to-back quick little rollers. Then I carved around six berms, multiple features, and did a little speed check. I knew a big jump we'd been overshooting in practice was coming up . . . *and* . . . *here it comes* . . . *YES!* I landed it. Trying to keep myself from gaining too much speed with the steepness, I navigated the last series of jumps and rollers. When I could see the finish, I got low, opened up and went as fast as possible. I hit the final jump and crossed the finish line. *Exhale.* I looked up at the clock. One minute, eight seconds.

I'd had a solid start and rode the course strong. That still wasn't fast enough to beat Bibian, who'd crossed the finish line a full eight seconds ahead of my official time. I was plenty aware that powerhouse Bibian would be tough to beat, but where the hell did the rider competing for France, Cécile Hernandez Cervellon, come from? She'd edged me out and was in second place. I'd raced against Cécile in some previous world cups and had always come out well ahead of her. In fact, in a race that season, I beat her by close to ten seconds. She had both her legs and a case of MS. She appeared to be having a great day.

"The snow is so challenging," I told my coach at the end of my first run. "I don't even want to push it because I don't want to risk falling."

"Just keep everything smooth and steady," he told me. "Sometimes riding smart is better then riding fast. Your time is still right up there in the top."

My second run was better, if only slightly. I crossed the line at one minute, six seconds. Meanwhile, as Bibian and Cécile seemed to keep a tight grip on the gold and silver slots and I struggled to hold on to a possible bronze, my teammates were having an even more difficult time. Because of the inconsistency of the snow and the pressure of the race, they were dealing with multiple slips, falls, tumbles, and sloppy toe edges. They all looked so bummed about how they were performing, and I gathered all my competitors in a circle. "You guys, I know this isn't going as well as we'd imagined," I said. "But on this last run, let's all be grateful for where we are. Don't forget, we are the best in the world, and we've trained our butts off to get here. Let's just stay in the moment, have fun, and enjoy every move. This is the last time there will ever be a first time!" We all high-fived.

Round three—the fight to keep my shot at the bronze. I steadied myself at the gate, drew in the deepest breath I could, closed my eyes, and again visualized the course. "This is it, Amy," I whispered to myself. "You've got this. Just do what you have been training to do." The start gate official looked in my eyes and said, "Are you ready?" "Let's do this," I said. He then started the countdown, "Five seconds, four, three, two, one . . ."—and then I was off. I hit the first few rollers, and then instead of a speed check, I decided to allow my edges to wash a little in the turns to just control my speed. I rode up over a steep roller . . . then off the dragon-back triple jump, and . . . *Yes!* I landed it beautifully. The words I'd left with my team-mates now reeled through my head. *Stay in the moment. Just have fun. Enjoy every move.* I cruised through one last stretch of rollers, opened up wide, hit the final bump, and blazed across the finish line. I pumped my fist in the air as I rode. I'm proud to say that I was the first female ever to bring home a bronze medal for Paralympic snowboarding. As I crossed the line, the crowd roared. Hundreds of camera flashes went off all around the stadium. Bibian, who was already at the finish line in tears, hugged me tightly. "We did it!" I told her, my own eyes filling with water.

That evening during the medal ceremony, a wave of emotion came over me. As I lowered my head so the official could place the bronze medallion around my neck, I felt overwhelmed with gratitude. I stood not just in representation of myself, or even of my sport. I also stood for any person who has ever been told that a victory isn't possible. For all those who've fought back from seemingly unbeatable odds. For every snowboarder who has ridden harder, dreamed bigger, and put everything on the line to pursue a passion. This was their medal. I was just the incredibly proud keeper of it.

As the U.S. flag was raised alongside the two others, the audience cheered. I stood there, taking it all in, with tears in my eyes. I reflected back on the road that had brought me here. I thought of that boy who once flew by me on his snowboard and made me curious enough to try this sport for the first time. I thought of the day a doctor told me I might not ever snowboard again—and another day when I nearly slipped away from this world to the next. I recalled the news we'd received in 2011 that snowboarding wouldn't even be part of these games. And yet, here I stood, on a podium. "Will I ever snowboard again?" I'd once fearfully asked a surgeon. My very presence at these games wasn't just an answer. It was a resounding yes. I closed my eyes, kissed the bronze that meant so much to me, and waved to the people below.

Right after the ceremony, Daniel and I found each other. He was holding a gorgeous bouquet of white tulips. "These are for you, baby," he said, embracing me. "Congratulations. You kicked ass."

My race looked nothing like I'd visualized. Yet I'd chosen to surrender to the course in front of me. Adapt to its evolving conditions. Control what I could—and surrender what I couldn't. When I thought about it, that's how I'd made it as far as I had in my life.

We don't always get to decide which course we go down or know which mountains we'll face. Yet we always have the most important choice there is: whether to resist, or to give ourselves over to the twists and turns of the terrain. As it goes in snowboarding, so it goes in life.

CHAPTER 18

Universal Rhythm

"Dancing with your feet is one thing,
but dancing with your heart is another."

—AUTHOR UNKNOWN

I didn't party much in Sochi. I shared a few toasts with Daniel and my teammates, but within hours of standing on that podium, I was on a plane to Los Angeles. Our big *Dancing with the Stars* premiere was in less than seventy-two hours, and we had yet to master our cha-cha. I hopped off the plane at 7 P.M., swung by the condo the show had set up for me, then raced to the studio to get there by nine. On Derek's final day in Russia, I'd asked him, "Do you think others have gotten as far as we have?" He laughed. "Um, yes, they've gotten farther," he said. "Some of them are working on their *second* dance." Damn.

In the large mirrored studio, Derek and I got down to business. I showed him what I recalled from Sochi. "Wow, you've remembered quite a bit!" he said. Once I'd shifted gears to snowboarding in Sochi, I'd had zero time to actually practice my dances. So I visualized them in the same way that I visualized my snowboard competitions, mapping out each move. In Sochi, I'd already done most of the steps at least once, in sections, but the whole dance hadn't yet been put together and set to music. That was our agenda that night.

The evening went well. I'd already come a long way with Derek's coaching, but there were still so many things I felt like I was missing. At midnight on the car ride home, I thought, *Are we really about to perform this dance before millions the day after tomorrow?* I found the thought both exciting and terrifying.

As much as I knew that I'd been brought on in part *because* of my legs, I was also surprised when they became the sole focus of attention. On my first day back in Los Angeles, just after rehearsal, Derek and I did a few press interviews. "What's it going to be like for you to dance in prosthetic legs? Are you really capable of that?" asked one interviewer. I answered as well as I could, but inside, I was thinking, *These legs do not define me. I am not my legs! And come on, guys, I just won a bronze in snowboarding. I think I'm pretty damn capable here.* I knew that—but it quickly became clear that I'd have to give the rest of the world a chance to catch up to my awareness.

I returned to the two-bedroom condo, which was clean and spacious. When I came through the door, gifts from the *DWTS* team awaited—cookies, jam, flowers, workout clothing, bottles of champagne. Some of my own sponsors also had gifts waiting for me: Element sent a gift basket of food, candles, and boxes of clothing; Toyota sent even more workout clothing. My parents were waiting for me at the condo. After sixteen hours of flying, followed by three hours of dancing, I was jet-lagged and delirious.

All the other teams had figured out their wardrobe for the pre-miere, as well as taken an official team photo. Derek and I squeezed all that into my second twenty-four hours in Los Angeles. A car picked me up from the condo at 6:30 A.M., and, still exhausted, I rode over to CBS. The wardrobe fitting was one of the coolest parts of the process. A producer led us to a building that was like its own tailoring shop; five rooms were filled with everything, from long rolls of colorful fabric and large spools of thread, to colorful hand-beaded outfits on mannequins. In one room, rows of seam-stresses sat lined up, sewing customized outfits for all of the danc-ers. I felt like I'd just walked into a very special and sparkly kingdom. In a way, that's what the entire show feels like. Every week, the team helps us create a fantasy and a new set of charac-ters to fully immerse ourselves in using costumes, makeup, and set design.

Did you know that every single outfit you see on *DWTS* is espe-cially created for each contestant? I found that fascinating. In the days leading up to the show, the dancers sit down with costume designers and actually sketch out ideas; in the weeks when a con-testant has two or three numbers, the team has to create two or three different options. *DWTS* is a major production, from the carefully planned set designs, to the makeup and wardrobe, to the live band and lighting, and what you see on television is only one very small portion of what's happening behind the scenes. Workers never seen by the public labor around the clock. I had one look around that place and thought, *This isn't just a little dance reality show. This is a massive production.*

I'd already given the producers my measurements. In Sochi,

Derek had asked, "What colors do you like? We need to start designing your cha-cha outfit." I hadn't given him much detail to work with, so he came up with a concept that went well with my dance: a fringy, beaded, gold-colored costume, complete with a little bralike top and pants with fringe on top of more fringe. "I'm telling you," Derek said, "with all your hip movement, the fringe on that outfit's going to look amazing." I tried it on, and once they'd made their alterations (several seamstresses began tucking, pinning, and sewing the outfit while I was still in it), I couldn't believe how well it fit. They weren't just tailors. They were *magicians*. They knew exactly how to pull in my waist and push up my boobs for maximum appeal.

Show day arrived. A car picked me up from the condo at 6:30 A.M.; my ABC call time for hair and makeup was at 7:30. Once there, I went to my personal *DWTS* trailer. It even had my name on the door; inside, there was even a robe with my name embroidered on it. The show also arranged for me to have an assistant, Michelle, on show days. By the hour, I was feeling more like a star. I hadn't expected any of this. "Anything you need," said Michelle, "just let me know," and that included energy bars, coconut water, food from the health food store, and of course, a set of tools to fix any sudden issues with my legs. At one point, I began jokingly calling Michelle my "leg handler."

First there's hair. Then there's makeup. Followed by an actual rehearsal on the elaborate set. "Turn this way instead," Derek told me as we practiced our routine onstage. "Wait, what? Are we changing things now? I'm barely hanging on to what I know!" I said. "I'm going to always be refining our performances until the minute we go onstage," Derek said. *Oh, really? Great.* There was so much to take in: the lights, the tweaks to the routine, how it feels to do your performance in front of producers. The pressure made me forget a couple of my steps. At least we got to rehearse our performances three times, and by the end, mine was better. Somewhat.

At the rehearsal, I saw some of the other contestants for the first time: Meryl. Candace. Charlie. Nene. Every team was called up over the loudspeaker, one at a time, to do their dance in front of the rest of us. Some of their dances were amazing enough to make me doubt whether I'd done enough practice, and Meryl, the ice champion, was of course flawless and spectacular. *How am I supposed to compete with an Olympic ice dancer—someone who's already considered one of the best dancers in the world? Well, she certainly will be keeping me on my toes. Literally.* I reminded myself that I just needed to stay in the moment, enjoy myself and see how far that would take me.

The other contestants were all nice, but because we'd started our training in Sochi, early on, I hadn't had much time to get to know them. When you do the show, your life exists in a triangle: Condo. Dance studio. CBS building. There's very little interaction with the outside world (other than through social media) and not as much hanging out among the other contestants as you might think. Everyone's off in their own triangle, too—and though we all shared the same rehearsal studios early on in the competition, I didn't cross paths with many. The night I arrived, I did run into James and Peta at the studio and we said a quick hello. And later, I got to know all of the contestants well, including Candace and Danica, and I've kept in touch with them and most of the others. Also, I loved Nene Leakes from *The Real Housewives of Atlanta*. She was so feisty, so fun. "Hey, girl!" she'd call out whenever she saw me on the set. Her husband and son were usually there with her.

As our curtain call inched closer, we were directed upstairs toward the skybox area, which is where all the dancers congregate, are interviewed by host Erin Andrews, receive their scores, and watch the other contestants' performances. When the cameras weren't on us, the hair and makeup team touched up our faces; other times, we'd do one last little practice on our dance. "You nervous?" Derek asked. "No, and that worries me a little," I said, laughing. Looking back on it, I think I was so nervous that I was numb. "Good," he said. "You're going to be totally fine." The idea that my family was there to support me did calm my nerves— they had flown in for the premiere.

At last, as we stood on opposite sides of the set, we heard our names over the loudspeaker: "Dancing the cha-cha-cha . . . Amy Purdy and her partner, Derek Hough!" I took one deep breath and thought, *This is it. No turning back.* In that second, the nerves hit. So I gave myself the same pep talk that I did in Sochi: "Amy, you've got this. Do what you have been training to do." The song "Counting Stars" by One Republic began. Then all at once, Derek and I strutted toward each other, with me counting out the steps in my head the entire time, "Five, six, seven, eight," just to stay on beat for us to meet in the center. We grabbed hands, did a few cha-cha twists, and the crowd went wild! As we cha-cha'd our way across the floor to the song's rhythm, my gold fringes twirling with every swing of my hips, the audience sang and clapped along to the lyrics: "Lately, I've been—I've been losing sleep, dreaming about the things we could be!" Then just like that, almost as quickly as it began, my first dance was done. Sweaty, I looked out to see everyone standing on their feet and cheering loudly. *Did we just do that?* Very surreal. And I couldn't believe I'd actually remembered the dance.

We then walked over to the judges, who gave us their feedback. I was just trying to catch my breath! High-intensity dancing is a serious workout, even when you're already in Olympic shape. "Let's clear one thing up from the start, Amy," said Len Goodman. "We can't judge you any differently than another star on the show—and I think that's how you'd like it." I nodded and agreed. "You got a bronze medal in the Olympics," he continued, "and you got a gold medal in the cha-cha-cha!" Next was Bruno Tonioli: "Beyond belief," he said. "We have Wonder Woman in this room—timing, shapes, performance level . . . how do you do it? I'm gobsmacked!" And last, the beautiful Carrie Ann Inaba: "I'm in shock," she said. "I've never seen anything like that. You are more than a dancer or contestant on this show. You are a beacon of light." In addition to being breathless, I was suddenly also speechless.

Upstairs, back in the skybox, we received the judges' scores: three 8's in a row, for 24 points out of a possible 30. Not bad for a girl with metal legs, little time to practice, and some serious jet lag. I knew the final result would be left up to the fans calling in to vote, and if folks at home felt even a little of the energy in the building, that could give me a chance. I suddenly understood why many of the contestants cry once they're done performing; it's such an intense emotional and physical experience. Less than a month earlier, I'd thought of an appearance on *DWTS* as something that would be "fun to try." It definitely is, but once you devote yourself to anything 100 percent, that level of passion elevates the entire experience from simply enjoyable to utterly exhilarating and fulfilling.

When I got back to the condo, my parents and sister, who were staying with me while they were in town, were all rewatching the show. "You were amazing, Amy, I can't believe it!" Crystal said. "You can really dance!" When I watched the recording with them, even I couldn't believe that was me on the screen.

Fans took note after that first dance. If my @AmyPurdyGurl Twitter page was on fire before, it went into a volcanic eruption at this point. Every Monday after the show, once I'd made my way through the long press line to do interviews and the other dancers had called it a night, I would go back to my trailer and set up a two-hour live Twitter chat. I wanted to talk to and thank my fans. Those sessions served as an immediate barometer of whether a performance had resonated. "I was crying so hard when I saw you and Derek do the cha cha," one viewer wrote. People of all ages reached out to me, but tweens, teens, and twenty-somethings seemed to show up in the most massive numbers. "Amy," one adorable nine-year-old wrote, "when I saw you dancing, it made me think, *If you she can do that, then I can get an A on my math test.* You are beyond inspiring!" Another wrote: "I've been trying to lose 50 pounds, and when I saw what you did, I joined the gym."

That first dance set the tone. I couldn't have known it then, but for nine more weeks, Derek and I would swing, waltz, tango, salsa, and quick-step our way into the lives and living rooms of millions and stay on top of the leaderboard. Not only had I gotten through my cha-cha; Derek and I had somehow managed to strike a nerve. Even as early as that first week, I recognized that this was about far more than just dancing. This was about transforming how people saw their very dreams and possibilities.

That shift was apparent even during the course of the season. Each week, I gave my extra tickets to a child with a disability, along with his or her family. One night after a show, Derek and I saw one of the kids I'd invited dancing out on the floor in her prosthetic legs. Derek looked at me and said, "That's what it's all about." "Yes," I responded. "It is." I didn't have someone in my situation to look up to when I lost my legs. What a privilege to be in a position to fill those shoes.

RESET—THAT'S WHAT DEREK taught me to do after each and every dance. "I got off beat at one point, and I think my shoulders were high," I told him after our first performance. "It's over," he told me. "It doesn't matter now. Put that dance in a box, lock it up, and throw away the key. We start on another one tomorrow." *Move on.*

From week to week, our work flow had its own rhythm. On Tuesdays, Derek would present me with the song the producers had chosen, often with his input. "Okay, are you ready to hear what we are going to dance to this week?" he'd always ask. How could I *not* be excited? I'd just finished an energizing performance the night before and still had a whole five days until the next one. After Derek played the song, he jumped right in and began experimenting with moves. Our Tuesday afternoons were just as busy: Over lunch, we met with the costume designers and gave them our ideas on set design and wardrobe so they could begin a sketch. Wednesday was all about learning multiple new segments of the dance, and by Thursday, Derek began piecing all those segments together into a full routine. Friday was an important day: That's when we had to record a wide-angle shot of our dance, along with the music, so that the producers, set designers, and other team members would have a clear idea of how to set us up on show day. Saturday, we did some major polishing, and Sundays, we performed the whole routine on the set. Then it all came down to Monday: hair and makeup, dress rehearsals, and a live taping of the show.

For ten weeks straight, that was my life. And those first weeks were the most intense of all. After rehearsals, I'd go do media interviews with TV shows like *Extra*. At one point, I'd been moving around so much that I couldn't even keep up with my own laundry, and I started running out of clean outfits to wear to these TV interviews. "Mom," I said one day by phone, "will you please come help me?" My amazing mother temporarily relocated from Boise to Los Angeles just to carry me through this experience with clean clothing and daily meals. Daniel and my dad, as well as some other relatives, flew in and out.

People often ask me, "What was the most challenging part of the competition for you?" Though my legs came with their challenges—like having my screws come loose right before a dance—surprisingly, that wasn't the most difficult part. It was learning the fundamentals of dance while balancing on these feet. I had to remember how to hold my shoulders down, pull from my lower lats, and move my arms gracefully. At times I would spend nearly an hour in the mirror, practicing moving my arms properly. At one point Derek looked over at me and laughed. "It's so cute watching you practice on your own," he said.

From the beginning, Derek told me, "I'm your wall, your stability." And he became just that, emotionally and physically. As I leaned on him, it made me realize how strong I'd been over the years. His leadership on the dance floor allowed me to surrender and connect with my femininity in a way that I never had. Looking back, I realized that when I lost my legs, I also felt like I lost part of what made me a woman. And through dance, I found it again. I will forever be grateful to Derek for helping me find that place again.

That femininity was on full display during the Disney week, which was one of the hardest weeks for me. We moved so slowly through the dance that I felt unstable in my legs—it felt like riding a bicycle in slow motion. I struggled through practice all week, the whole time wondering if it would be the dance that would finally take us out of the competition. It was frustrating and emotional. Having had ankles for nearly twenty years, I knew how they were supposed to be moving, yet I wasn't able to move them that way. For the first time during the competition, my strong "I can do anything" attitude fell apart and I truly allowed myself to break down. Once I'd wiped away the tears, I realized that like I had done so many times before, I had to work harder and find a way to overcome. And by the end of the week, I did: I stepped out of my snowboard gear and into a ballroom gown and waltzed out as Cinderella. As Derek, my Prince Charming, guided me across the floor, I truly felt like a beautiful princess! That week and on so many others, I got to live out a new character and fantasy. It felt like a dream.

I loved all the dances, but my all-time favorite was the contemporary dance. The producers gave us the theme ahead of time: "the most memorable year of your life." "So what are your thoughts on that theme?" Derek asked. We were seated in the studio. "Well, obviously, losing my legs and getting the kidney from my father are memorable, but this year is also pretty memorable with med-aling at the Paralympics," I said.

To be honest, I didn't really want to talk about the past. Yes, I'd opened up about that in speeches, but for a dance show? I hadn't planned to go that deep. And besides that, I'd moved so far past that period of my life. "I know it's going to be vulnerable," Derek told me, "but I think you should go there. The story of what you went through and how far you've come is what's going to inspire people. But it's your choice." After a lot of back-and-forth with Derek, I chose to open up. I would pay tribute to my dad for his incredible gift of a kidney. Through the flow of the dance, Derek and I would tell the story of me falling—and my father always being there to catch me. I told my parents I wanted them to be at the next show. I just didn't reveal exactly why.

Derek chose our song. One afternoon as he ran on the tread-mill at his hotel in Sochi, the song "Human" by Christina Perri came on the radio. "I thought it was such a beautiful song, so pow-erful," Derek told me that Tuesday. The song, he explained, is about how vulnerable each of us is—"I bleed when I fall down . . . I crash and I break down." "I immediately thought about your story when I heard it," he said. "Do you know it?" I didn't. "Let me play it for you." He did, and by the last note, we both needed the Kleenex. "What do you think? Do you like it?" I nodded and tried to hold back another round of gushing tears.

For this dance in particular, I wanted to look beautiful and feminine, with nice lines to my legs . . . as in pointed toes. "I have an idea!" I said. "One of the leg manufacturers that sponsors me, Freedom Innovations, has these swimming feet that are pointed. I

don't know if I can balance on them but we could try?" Derek
liked that idea, but even as I suggested it, I wasn't sure the feet
would work; they're made to have a flipper put on them for scuba
diving, not dancing. I called the leg manufacturer to get some
details. "Do you think these are strong enough to stand on the tips
of the toes? Could I walk on the tippy-toes in these?" Their answer:
The feet were *supposed* to be able to hold up to two hundred
pounds—but they weren't completely sure they would, given that
the tips of the toes weren't made to be stood on. The only way I
could know for sure was to test them—so I had my leg manufacturer overnight them.

"Whoa, those are amazing," said Derek the first he saw me in
them. I could indeed stand in them; it was just really tough to
stay balanced, because remember, I was on the absolute point of
my toes. I took a few steps and wobbled. "The lines are *gorgeous*," Derek said. When I sat in them, they made me feel so
girly. I could cross my legs, let my foot drop, and have my toe
pointed downward, making my legs look long and lean. That
might seem like a small thing, but it's exactly the kind of feminine gesture you miss after you've lost your legs. Ultimately, we
chose to use the feet.

The entire week leading up to the show was as physically
draining as it was emotional. Right alongside Derek's artistic
genius is his tendency to shift all over the place: One minute, he's
emotional (we cried together multiple times that week while developing the dance). The next moment, he's belting out a song at the
very top of his lungs. Or he'd be laughing his ass off and cracking
jokes and making our producer and me laugh just as hard. And
some of the time, he was just plain exhausted. I was fascinated

and inspired by his expressiveness. And in addition to working with me, Derek was preparing to go on a huge dance tour across the country, so he was under major pressure.

In week three, the studio was overflowing with intensity, because of the high emotions of the dance we were working on. "I need you to turn *this* way," Derek would say, demonstrating. And if I didn't do it right after a few tries, he was understandably frustrated. But here's the side of Derek I loved: He's a guy who's always working on himself. If he seemed cantankerous one moment, he was completely capable of coming back the next and saying, "Wow, I see why you're struggling with this part of the dance. It's because I didn't bring the right energy into the room when I taught it to you." I truly appreciated him telling me that. One of my favorite quotes is "Leaders are learners." Derek embodied that idea. He was such a brilliant leader because he is always willing to learn and grow. And early on, it was also clear to me that Derek was a special person, that he was connected to something much bigger than himself. His ideas flowed freely. He was so expressive; his channels to God or the universal energy were wide open. He was and is a bottomless pit of energy, talent, and ideas.

By Thursday of the tribute week, we'd nailed down much of the performance. "If I were your dad," Derek had told me in rehearsals, "this is how I would hold you." He then let me lean on him during the most poignant part of the song. By this point, we'd figured out that the swimming feet worked, and I was strong enough to walk around and balance on them. Yet I was still a little wobbly, and the hardest part of the dance would be when I had to let go of Derek's hand and just stand there on my own two tippy-toes.

On Friday when we did our wide-angle shot, Derek dimmed the lights in the studio. We then performed the dance from start to finish, and the emotion in that room was palpable. "If we can get through this on Monday," I told Derek, "it's going to be spectacular." Derek didn't like when I put too much pressure on myself, so he reminded me, "It will be spectacular no matter what."

Monday rolled around. Backstage, Derek, who's a fan of the motivational speaker Tony Robbins, would always use some of what he'd learned at Tony's conferences to help me on show day. On this night, we pressed our foreheads together and breathed deeply for a minute—a way to get grounded in the moment. "You're going to hear the taped package with your story in it," he told me. "You're going to see your dad in the audience and the music's going to start—and that's all going to be incredibly emotional. You need to use this emotion as strength." I nodded and recalled all the times I'd done exactly that in my acting, speaking, and snowboard races.

Before this show and others, Derek and I also did what he called "stacking." He placed his hand over my heart and said, "Okay, think of something that you're grateful for." "Well," I said, "I'm grateful to have the chance to say thank you to my dad." He then took my hand and stacked it over his hand and said, "I'm grateful to be dancing with you, Amy." We kept stacking and stacking, and at the end of it, we'd surrounded ourselves with the powerful energy of gratitude to take with us onto the stage. Up in the skybox, about a minute before the producers called us to the stage, Derek leaned and whispered to me: "You weren't even supposed to be walking, and now you're *dancing*. So just remember: You have already won, no matter what happens, every single step you take is perfect." He always knew how to make me feel relaxed and confident before a performance.

We took our places on the stage. I began in a seated position on the floor, resting my cheek on my knees. Derek came up from the side, leaned over, and gently lifted me from the ground. The first few notes of the song began, and Derek guided me forward as I balanced on the tips of my toes. "I can hold my breath," the song played. Derek lifted me up into the air as I swung my legs overhead. "I can bite my tongue." I took three steps forward on my perfectly pointed feet, and Derek and I came together, holding hands and facing each other. Then in the hardest move for me, the climax of the song, he let my hands go, and I pushed off him, standing tall. The stage lights fanned across my body as I balanced perfectly on my toes, using every bit of energy in my body to stabilize myself. A moment later, I moved into Derek's arms, he picked me up, and he spun me in the air with the lights of the stage opening up like a flower. The energy was so intense for the two of us, and it's hard to describe the amount of gratitude I felt in that moment. Then at last, the final refrain: "I'm only human." As the audience stood to its feet and applauded with tears in their eyes, I looked over and saw my father. He was dabbing away tears. I left the stage and rushed over to embrace him, and as he held me, I whispered this into his ear: "Thank you, Dad—thank you."

By the time the judges gave their comments, a mix of mascara and tears stained my face as I tried to keep my composure long enough to get backstage again. "I hope you know what you're doing for people, when they see you dance every week," said Robin Roberts, the *Good Morning America* anchor who served as a guest judge that evening. "For anyone who's facing a challenge, you are letting them know that they, too—*we, too*—can begin again anew." And that's when I lost it. Because Robin's words that evening were a confirmation of exactly what Derek and I set out to do: help others recognize their own power by watching me step into mine.

"WHO'S YOUR ICON, Amy?" my producer, Alex, stopped by the studio to ask me one morning around week eight. He was already preparing for week nine, the American Icon week—and he and the other producers were clearly trying to line up potential guests.

"My icon?" I said, wrinkling my forehead.

"Yes, your icon," he said. "Who would you pick?"

"Gosh, I don't really know. I mean the only famous person I have ever truly looked up to is Oprah." I mean, there were artists, athletes, and musicians that I loved, but Oprah was the only person I could think of who truly inspired me to my core.

"Oprah Winfrey?" he said. He nearly dropped the pad he was writing on.

"Yes. Oprah," I said. "I'd go with Oprah. She has overcome huge obstacles in her life. And she has changed people's lives by giving back."

He sucked in a slow breath. "Well, okay," he finally said. "There's no way we are getting Oprah on the show. Got anyone else who's a little less 'Oprah'?"

"Nope," I said. "That's it. Just Oprah."

The producer left. I thought, *He's right: They are never going to get her on the show.* Frankly, after the producer asked me about it, I put the conversation out of my head and moved on to the task at hand: learning my quickstep.

Derek and I had amazed even ourselves that I was still in the show by week eight. I had proven that I could dance and that I deserved to be there. But stepping foot into the competition, who would've ever thought we'd make it so far? If you had any idea what we had to *do* in order to keep competitive (those taped pieces they show leading up to the live dances are just a very thin slice of what happens in the studio every day! We danced up to six hours a day, seven days a week without a day off), it would be enough to make you crave a long nap. Even I need one when I think back on it. But to be honest, I loved every moment of it.

First of all, I used four different sets of feet during the entire season—none of which moved the way normal feet move, and none of which are actually made for dancing. We didn't have anything to go off of when deciding which pair of feet would work for which dance. By experimenting with feet and body movements, week by week, we paved our own path. We ultimately settled on four pairs: There were my usual high-heel everyday walking feet (having a heel they worked best for the swing, and waltz); my Sach feet (they were made of wood and foam and had zero ankle motion or dynamic movement; they were basically mannequin feet, however, they had a nice shaped arch; we found that when I didn't wear shoes, I was able to balance on the balls of the my feet, which allowed me to move my hips for the Latin dances, like the salsa jive and rumba). I also had my swimming feet (those stilts I balanced on in our contemporary dance and the Argentine tango); and then, of course, the week nine feet—those fierce running blades I used to propel myself forward and side to side during the quickstep. Who knew you could do the quickstep on running blades? Now we know! After our quickstep aired, many parents uploaded videos of their kids dancing in their running legs while watching Derek and me dance on television. It truly was amazing to see and so heartwarming.

"Which is harder—*Dancing with the Stars* or competing in the Paralympics?" others have often asked me. I always say *DWTS*. With snowboarding, once I figured out I could do it, I was able to build on my skill set and refine my legs; that allowed me to get better, faster, and stronger by the week. But with the show, each and every week was different, and in my case, the feet I used and ankle motion I needed to master were also different. So with every dance, we had to completely go back to the drawing board and cross our fingers that we would figure it out. We always did. That's a lesson I've carried away from my experience on the show: There's always a way, if we're willing to try hard enough to find it.

ONE DAY IN the studio as we were preparing to get started on the quickstep routine, my producer brought me a phone. "You'll need this today," he said. "Someone's going to call you." I grinned, but then I thought, *No way is it going to be Oprah.*

I was wrong. An hour later, the cell phone rang. It was Oprah. I could not even believe it. I put her on speakerphone so Derek could hear, and this is just a portion of our conversation:

"Hello, is this Amy?" I knew the voice, *but was this real*?

"Hi, yes," I said, my voice quivering a little. "This is Amy."

"Hi, Amy. This is Oprah."

"Are you serious?" I placed my hand over my heart. "Oh my God!"

Derek piped in: "Hi, Oprah, how are you doing?"

"Is that Derek?"

"It is!"

"Oh my gosh, it's both of you," Oprah said.

"Wow, we're surprised to hear from you," said Derek, while my mind was still racing for just what to say. "It's amazing."

"You all are so inspiring," Oprah said. "If you look up the word *inspiring* in the dictionary, your photos would be right there. And Amy, I just got to tell you—unbelievable. I don't even know how you're doing what you're doing."

"I don't, either!" I said. "This is so exciting, my hand is shaking."

"So I'm telling you, when you win, I'm going to take you both out to dinner. I promise. I'll be watching!" Oprah said. On the episode, the conversation lasted less than a minute, but in real life, it lasted about ten. I was amazed that I was even on the show, much less on the phone with Oprah! The second we hung up, I let out a huge scream.

That week, we rocked the house. One very fast quickstep on blades—and thanks to Oprah, one chick with a full heart.

WE MADE IT to the finale. In the hours leading up to the night of the big mirror ball presentation, we had our last massive push of work. The finale is a two-night event, and on the first of those two nights, we were to perform two dances: the salsa and the freestyle. If we made it through eliminations, we would move on to the 24-hour challenge, meaning that after dancing that day, we would head back to the rehearsal studio that evening and choreograph our final dance to be performed the second night. In our case, that would be a fusion of dance styles: the Argentine tango and the cha-cha. "This competition could really go in either direction," Derek told me. "You've proven that you're an amazing dancer, and you've worked your ass off harder than anyone. But Meryl and Max are stunning, and the taped packages are making me think some viewers want to vote for them even more so. I just have a feeling."

This was probably Derek's way of trying to lessen the blow for me if we didn't win. But in a way, that thought freed us to do exactly what we'd been doing for nine weeks—writing our own script. Making our own rules. And performing on our terms. In our minds, we had already won more than a trophy. We had experienced more and went farther together than we could've ever imagined. Win or lose, our intention was to leave our viewers with one statement of possibility in the form of a dance. We chose the freestyle as that dance.

"Do you have any idea for a freestyle song?" he asked me. The producers had been asking us for weeks, and we'd had no idea. We wanted to stay present in the moment and not think that far ahead. But as the finale approached and we settled on the idea that we'd use our dance for a larger purpose, one that we felt could transcend even the show, we started brainstorming. "I want something that says 'The sky's the limit,'" Derek said. I loved that.

Although we didn't yet have a song, I wasn't worried—just as we had every week, I knew we'd find the right one. I trusted that Derek would have another one of his *aha* moments, and a day later, he did. He got into his car, turned the radio on, and heard the song "Dare You" by Hardwell. The lyrics sounded as if they'd been written for me. "I dare you to love, I dare you to cry, I dare you to run." That was it. "No words better defined our experience on the show for ten weeks," he told me as he played it. I agreed. We had our song. Now we just needed a dance to go along with it.

"I want you to see something," Derek texted me one night. He included a link to a YouTube video. When I clicked on it, I saw a video of an aerialist, hanging from a rope and spinning fifteen feet up in the air. When I saw Derek later, I said, "That was cool," and I had a good idea of where this was going. By this time, I knew Derek well. "I want you to do that move," he said. "That's how we should end our dance." It looked difficult, and very nauseating, but I didn't argue. That's the thing about getting to week ten: Nine weeks in a row, you've already proven to yourself that whatever looked downright impossible on a Tuesday can become a reality six short days later. "Okay," I said. "Let's try it."

Derek and I went to a local aerial studio in Los Angeles to see a friend of his, Angel. "Amy, did Derek show you the video of what he wants you to do?" he said, smiling. "Yes," I said, glancing over at Derek. He was smiling as well. *What is he not telling me?* "Well, it usually takes at least a couple of weeks to build up enough upper-body strength to do that move," he said. Derek cut in: "Well, buddy, we don't have a few weeks, we have about an hour to figure out if she can do this before we get back to the rehearsal studio." Derek glanced over to see the worried expression on my face. "Amy," he said, "I know you got this."

Angel took me over to an area of the studio with a trapeze. We did a few warm-ups, and then he said, "I'm going to have you do some pull-ups on the trapeze." I put my hands on the bar, inhaled, and lifted my legs straight out in front of me so my body was at a

90-degree angle. Hello—major ab work. I pulled myself up into a pull-up position. "Can you do five pull-ups?" he said. I did. He then asked me to drop one arm at a time and do five pull-ups on each. *Aaaaagh*. "You got this, Amy," Derek cheered. "Go, go, go!" I got through it, and afterward, I dropped to the floor in a full sweat. "Oh my God," I said, out of breath, "was that *supposed* to be that hard?" My lats and entire midsection were quivering. Angel shot Derek a look. "Um, that was completely amazing," said Angel. "You're going to have no problem with this." And my training for the Paralympics was paying off.

In the middle of all this, Derek and I were also practicing our salsa—for the finale, we had to learn multiple dances at once. And though the freestyle was to be our last statement, Derek was nonetheless determined to make all three of our last dances spectacular—he filled the routines with lifts and moves more difficult and spectacular than any we'd performed previously. It was all very fun, until the morning when, while rehearsing our salsa dance, I—*crack!*—heard a pop in my rib cage. My whole upper back went into a full spasm. "Oh my God," I said, falling to my knees. The exact same thing had happened before during my rumba dance; an ambulance had to rush me to the hospital. We called in the chiropractor right away. He popped my rib back into place and told me I needed to immediately ice it to get the swelling and spasm to relax. It'll be extremely sore," he told me afterward, "but nothing's broken. It'll be up to you whether you can work through the pain."

At this point, we were only three days away from the finale, and the only part of my freestyle I'd worked on was that hanging rope spin. No other part of the dance had been touched. Meanwhile, Derek was pacing nervously. He was leaving on his dance tour within days of the finale—and there I was, seventy-two hours away from our final dance, wrapped in ice and downing ibuprofen. That's when Derek looked at me and said, "What do you think? Can we pull this off?"

I shrugged. "I don't know," I said.

"Well, look," he finally said. "You're in a lot of pain. We need to finish the freestyle and we can't be gentle. We need to practice all the lifts so we know we can do it. Plus, we haven't even finished our other dances. Should we call it?" Knowing that he was just overwhelmed, I shot back with "Call it? There's no way! We've come too far!!"

"Okay," he said, "but there isn't time to be injured. We have to finish these dances tonight."

"Give me a few hours," I said. "I'll go home, lay on ice, and let you know my answer later. I just need some time to regroup." And given the amount of pressure he was under, so did he. Every moment he wasn't with me, he was practicing for his tour.

Driving home that afternoon, the pain was so severe that I thought *I have no idea how I'm going to make it through this.* After all the hard work we'd put in to get so far, I was devastated that an injury might be the reason I couldn't complete the competition. But it's amazing the amount of strength you can find when you're forced to do so. I went home, took some ibuprofen, and laid on the floor on frozen ice packs for three hours. I simply made a choice: No matter what amount of pain I was in, I was going to dig deep and finish what I started. I texted Derek. "Let's do this," I wrote. "See you in thirty minutes."

That night, in the latest and most painful rehearsals I had ever endured, we developed our freestyle dance. Every. Single. Step of it. Once we'd finished at a little past midnight, a producer shot our wide video to send to the stage directors. Derek looked right into the camera and introduced the dance this way: "This is our free-style," he said, explaining how the dance would be set up. "We literally just came up with this dance right now. Amy is injured. Cross your fingers that we can pull this thing off. May God be with us." We then did the dance on tape—not amazingly well, but we got through it. And I knew that if I could muster the will and the strength to make it through that night, then I could make it through the finale itself.

On the evening of the freestyle, I made a goal for myself. Since this was to be one of my last dances, I wanted to fully enjoy every single moment. We began our dance by standing back-to-back, and there was something so powerful about the stillness of that first moment. We were present with each other. I could feel the energy and focus from the audience. Then the announcer finally said our names: "Amy Purdy, and her partner, Derek Hough." I felt calmer than I ever had. I took a few deep breaths and one last thought went through my mind before the music began: *No matter what happens, this is going to be perfect.*

And it was. There's a connection you share with your partner when you dance, and by this time, I had full trust in Derek. I was able to just let go, which allowed me to be fully in the moment. With millions watching, Derek and I moved precisely in tune with each other. I did not just dance. With every piece of my soul, I felt as if I moved to the universal rhythm that connects us all. I could hear the music more clearly than I had ever heard it throughout the season. For once, my body was moving, but my mind was still.

I didn't think about the beats or counts or what step was coming next. I just flowed with the melody; it was as if someone had pressed the play button and my body knew exactly what to do.

As Derek lifted me into the air and I clung to the rope with one hand, I didn't just defy gravity. I defied every doubt I'd ever had of myself, demonstrating the capacity we all have to do more. Rise higher. Push past boundaries. As I spun, my heart overflowed with gratitude. For the millions who supported me. For Derek's friendship and coaching. For Daniel and my family, whose love has seen me through my journey. For the strength in my body. And for each and every experience I'd had—yes, even the tough ones—that led me to this moment. For the courage I'd called upon to carry me from losing my legs to finding my wings.

The following night, Max and Meryl won the competition—Derek had correctly predicted that. As hard as we'd fought to win, we were sincerely happy for their triumph. For the first time, Max had led his dance partner to a win—and Meryl, who brought so much amazing talent to the ballroom floor, earned the top prize; what an honor and an accomplishment to come in second place to the best ice dancer in the world! In the last episode, the presentation of the mirror ball trophy was the show's defining moment. Yet just one night earlier, in an experience I will remember for the rest of my life, I had already created my own.

Reflections

"It is love alone that gives worth to all things."
—ST. TERESA OF ÁVILA

My path has led me to the perfect place. I truly believe that I'm standing exactly where I should be at this juncture in my life. Every step of my journey, even the most heartrending ones, was meant to happen. Each person I've connected with has come into my life for a reason. There are no coincidences. No mistakes. No accidents. There are only learning experiences, and each one can be used as a powerful lesson in moving forward.

I'm not suggesting that we should somehow celebrate crisis. Life often brings tremendous sorrow, tragedy, and loss. As we should, we weep. We feel overwhelmed. We raise our voices and our fists in complete agony. We bow our heads and wish so badly that the blow could be softened. I have lived through that kind of devastation. I once reckoned with the fear that I'd not only lose my legs, but also my life.

Yet once the initial intensity of that anguish has lessened—once days have settled into months, and months have thrust us squarely in the face of a new reality—we always have a choice. Our lives are not determined by what happens to us, but by how we *respond* to what happens to us. We can either see our circumstances as a set of random cruelties and then allow those hardships to turn us into bitter victims; or we can recognize the fact that, though we may never comprehend why hard things happen, they do, and when they do, we can reach for a larger purpose beyond the pain. After surviving the loss of my legs and full kidney failure, that is what I have chosen to do.

Each of us is energy. And whether or not we know it, we are constantly giving and receiving energy. That energy has the power to either harm or heal. "All human actions are motivated at their deepest level by two emotions—fear or love," Neale Donald Walsch wrote in *Conversations with God*. "In truth, there are only two emotions, only two words in the language of the soul. Fear wraps our bodies in clothing. Love allows us to stand naked. . . . Fear attacks. Love amends."

I've come to realize that my larger purpose—that persistent whisper that has compelled me toward "something more" for most of my life—is really about sharing love with others and becoming the highest expression of myself. While I was having the spleen surgery, Dr. Abby whispered a sentence to me that I will always remember: "Whatever it is you believe in, Amy, think about that now." At the time, I couldn't answer him because I was under such heavy anesthesia. But if a response were possible, I would have said this: "I believe in love."

The stage from which I can offer that positive energy has gotten bigger as my dreams have evolved. But I don't need a grand stage from which to share my passions, my inspirations, and my talents. None of us does. In the smallest interactions—a kind word to a friend, a smile to a passerby, a gesture of compassion to even a stranger—we have many opportunities to care for one another, as well as to use our lives and our gifts to the fullest extent.

Love comes in various forms. In fact, the word *love* is so layered that the Greeks created multiple words to distinguish its types. Among the many, there's *eros* (a passionate, romantic, and deeply emotional love); *philos* (the fondness and loyalty we usually feel for friends and family); and *agape* (a spiritual, selfless love we can offer humankind). I have experienced all three.

When it comes to romantic love, what Daniel and I have shared is so much more meaningful to me than the superficial, roses-and-chocolate version of love that our culture often highlights. We've had major ups and downs. Yet through more than a decade of falling down, getting up, and reconnecting, we've developed a genuine love, a deep respect, and a full acceptance of one another. Whatever happens in our relationship, I know those things will last.

Literally every day, I whisper a prayer of thanks to my mom, my dad, Crystal, and every friend and family member who has stood by me; *philos* is almost too small a word to express my overwhelming gratitude for their support. *Philos* is also the sort of love I've had with Derek. During our time together on the show, I was inspired by his boundless artistic expression, his incredible work ethic and passion, and his ability to transform a seemingly disconnected set of steps into a brilliant masterpiece. Just being around him made me want to stretch myself. Derek's very existence is evidence that we're all capable of more than we can conceive.

Agape—that's the unconditional love for others that I aspire to daily. It's not just a form of sharing; it's a way of *being*. Our lives come down to offering as much love as we can to the people around us, whether that love comes in the form of *agape*, or any of the others. Love, and my desire to express and experience it, is why I believe I was given a second chance. It's why the silhouetted beings offered me a choice to return. It's ultimately what the stranger meant when he spoke of trading a surface life for one on a completely different vibration. It's what the curly-haired man was trying to tell me when he repeated, "The only way is the shaman way," the path of healing. In my view, love is the only thing that will surely make sense in the end. That's not only true for me—it's true for every person on the earth. A fulfilling life isn't based on what we have or don't have; it's based on what we give of ourselves.

I've also discovered a fourth kind of love—the love for life itself and the passion we bring to everything we do. You could call this the love of inspiration and creativity. It's that profound sense of connection we feel when we completely give ourselves over to a project, a goal, a calling. When we immerse ourselves in this way, what we produce literally creates the world around us. This is the love that has lit my path. It has motivated me to keep striving. Changing. Giving. Growing. And pushing myself to do better in ways both big and small.

Every human being is a walking, talking, breathing set of lessons, and my lessons have been plentiful. I've learned the importance of building and sustaining dreams—of visualizing myself in the next chapter of my adventure even as I enjoy the one I'm in. I was born a dreamer; you may have been as well. But as the pressures of our world overwhelm us, those stresses often eclipse our vision of what's possible. Time and again, I've had to renew my vision. Reaffix my gaze on the potential for the miraculous. Seek out new ways to turn the mundane into the magical. That takes practice, and I've had plenty of it. A vision is a seed. When that seed receives the water of consistent effort, our lives can begin to blossom.

Nearly anything is possible. We hear that sentence a lot, but in my life, those aren't just words. They are a daily reality. Life has taught me that if you're passionate and willing to work hard, you can rise above some of the most bleak situations. And even when a circumstance can't be changed, we can alter our perception of it.

In my journey, I've endured some serious setbacks, and I'm not just here—I'm thriving. The challenges, the obstacles, the so-called barriers—they have all become stepping-stones I've used to make my way toward my goals. My biggest struggles have led to my biggest accomplishments. I believe in the power of intention, and when I look back on my life, I realize that my intention has always been to find a way, whether that's by learning how to snowboard again, or figuring out how to dance, or making a career out of motivational speaking.

The number one question people ask me is, "What's the thing that has helped you through the darkest times?" My answer has always been the same: gratitude. Focusing on what I have versus focusing on what I don't have. Being thankful for everything, even in moments when it seems we have nothing. No matter how hard things have gotten, I've continued to move forward, and I am absolutely convinced that you can do the same. I don't possess some kind of special power that sets me apart from humanity. We were all born with a capacity for greatness that far exceeds our wildest imagination.

Since *Dancing with the Stars* aired, people have often come up to me and said, "You are so inspiring." I always thank them for their kindness, but the truth is that I didn't go on the show or do anything else in my life with the sole intention of being inspiring. I'm just living out my passion. When we see others doing what they were meant to do, we are inspired to do the same. It's contagious. And the very fact that we can recognize and be inspired by that passion is a sign that we also possess it.

My legs haven't disabled me. If anything, they've enabled me. They've planted my feet on the spiritual path I was meant to walk. They've forced me to get creative. They've taught me that when I fall down, I can either lie there and wallow in my misstep, or I can use the experience as fuel for growth. I may have lost the legs of flesh and bone that I was born with, but these legs made of carbon fiber and rusted bolts have taken me to amazing places. And though my journey has looked pretty different from the one I thought I'd take, I've still done exactly what I set out to do. I've snowboarded. I've traveled. I've even cha-cha'd, quickstepped, and tangoed. And along the way, I've shared my life with some amazing people I never even imagined I'd meet, like Oprah. As it turns out, I not only received that call from her on *Dancing with the Stars*, but I also later joined her on a tour across the country. What an incredible full-circle moment, especially after so many years of feeling inspired by her work.

The question I first asked myself back in 1999 is the one I'm still asking: "If my life were a book, and I was the author, how would I want my story to go?" Each morning, I wake up grateful for another chance to add a page to my adventure. If the life I've already been blessed with is a sign of what's to come, then there will be many more fascinating chapters. One day at a time—one *dream* at a time—I'm still busy writing.

Acknowledgments

When I think about all those who've been part of my journey, one word comes to mind: gratitude. I am deeply thankful for the many people, both named and unnamed, who have come alongside me with their love, support, and encouragement. Here are a few I'd like to thank publicly:

Mom: Thank you for being the woman I have always looked up to and hoped to become myself.

Dad: Thank you for giving me life twice. I hope I am making you proud.

Crystal: You are my angel and I love you.

Daniel: Thank you for being my best friend, my business partner, and my love through some of the toughest challenges and greatest accomplishments of my life. I am grateful to share this journey with you.

Keith Dahl of Toyota: Thank you for helping my life come full circle. I would not be doing what I am today if it wasn't for your belief in me.

Johnny and Kori Schillereff of Element Skateboards: Thank you for your friendship, and for believing in me from the very beginning.

Nancy Gale: I'm grateful for your rigorous work on Adaptive Action Sports. Our organization would not be where it is today without all of your blood, sweat, and tears.

GG and Pops: Thank you for your love, and for instilling in me a love of the outdoors.

My aunt Cindy and aunt Debbie, my cousins Michelle, Jack, Shannon and Jessica, and my niece Bryten, and my nephew Jonas: You are my best friends in life, and I appreciate you.

My uncle Stan: Thank you for always being there to protect me.

My close girlfriends Jina, Michelle, and Charlet: I will always be thankful for our lifelong connection.

Rob Gurdison, Josh Hetzle, Seamus Little, Mark Idol, Johnny Black, Dan Zavala, and Austin Spencer: Thank you for your friendship through some of the hardest years of my life.

Miah Wheeler: You've taught me how riding smart is riding fast. I appreciate you.

Evan Strong: Every day, you've inspired me to live a whole and healthy life.

My Team USA teammates: Thank you for your friendship, for your passion, and for keeping me on my toes. Because of you, I am the athlete I am today.

Derek Hough: Thank you for being my coach, my friend, and my wall on the dance floor—and for creating a safe place for me to grow. You have confirmed in me all that I am and want to be.

Dr. Abby: Thank you for giving me a second chance at life.

Barbara Seymour Giordano: You've been my speaking coach, my life coach, and my friend for life—and I am thankful.

My agents, Patrick Quinn & Jeannie Goldstein: Thank you for your support and guidance. It means a lot.

My coauthor, Michelle Burford: Thank you for bringing to life the story I've wanted to share for so many years.

Oprah: Thank you for inspiring me through your work and for your belief in me.

God, Mother Nature, the universe, Buddha, whoever is up there and holds the power: for giving me the choice to come back and live.

Shane Bird at Canyon Ranch: Thank you for your friendship through the toughest days.

The ICU nurses: Thank you for all the tedious hard work. I credit you for much of my survival.

My trainer, David Tittle: Thank you for helping me crush my own limitations.

Deena Katz of *DWTS*: Thank you for seeing the potential in me and for taking a risk. None of us knew what to expect when I stepped foot on that dance floor. Your support brought me to where I stand today.

My prosthetists, Kevin Bidwell and Stan Patterson: Thank you for your love, hard work, patience and belief in me. You both got me in the legs that have taken me to so many places! I know I can be particular, especially about shoes, so thank you for putting up with me!

And of course, none of this would've been accomplished without the skills of my team at HarperCollins. Thanks to Lisa Sharkey, who signed me up; Amy Bendell, who has invested hours on the manuscript; and Paige Hazzan, who has pored over the details. Much appreciation and excitement also goes to the Art Director, Photo Editor, marketing team, and the extraordinary sales force at HarperCollins. I am very appreciative of your enthusiasm and support.